AUTOMOBILES OF THE
FIFTIES

AUTOMOBILES OF THE
FIFTIES

Edited by
WP Jennings

MALLARD PRESS

First published in the United States of
America in 1991 by The Mallard Press.
Mallard Press and its accompanying design
and logo are trademarks of BDD Promotional Company, Inc.

ISBN 0-792-45584-3

Printed in Hong Kong

Designed by Tom Debolski
Captioned by Timothy Jacobs

All pictures are courtesy of the respective
manufacturers with the following
exceptions:
American Graphic Systems Picture
    Archives 6, 9 (right), 10 (left), 16 (left), 21
    (right), 33 (top), 39 (right), 46, 47, 61 (bot-
    tom), 62, 72, 73, 81, 82, 84 (left), 90, 98,
    110 (top)
Neill Bruce 121
Andrew Clarke Collection 126, 127
CW Editorial 120
© Tom Debolski 51 (top), 64, 65, 68 (top),
    113 (bottom)
Haymarket Motoring Picture Library 119
    (top)
© W Jeanne Kidd 79
© Wm T Randol 55, 91
Nicky Wright 117, 118, 119 (bottom), 122-123
    (both), 124-125 (both)
© Bill Yenne 14, 50, 51 (bottom), 58, 59, 63,
    66 (all), 67, 70, 71, 74, 75, 78, 89, 94, 96
    (left), 101, 106 (left), 110 (bottom), 111

Page 1: **A 1958 Buick Century, with the
kind of styling that dominated the late
1950s.**

Page 2: **This 1957 Corvette, with a 283 ci
(4.6 L) V-8 and Venetian Red paint job,
was (and is) a classic.**

At left: Suburbia welcomed the clean lines
of such as this 1954 Ford Mainline sedan,
in a sleek coat of gray.

CONTENTS

DENIED, DEPRIVED, AND DEPRAVED   6

CITIES, SUBURBS AND THE
   COUNTRY SQUIRE   22

POWER STEERING, THE AUTOMATIC
   TRANSMISSION AND WOMEN   34

WHITE BUCKS AND SADDLE SHOES   48

CHOPPED, CHANNELED AND
   CUSTOMIZED   62

DAYTONA, BONNEVILLE AND
   POINTS SOUTH   76

THE CREAM OF THE CROP   90

HOT WHEELS   100

THE FRUGAL, THE FAST AND
   THE FINE   116

INDEX   128

DENIED, DEPRIVED AND DEPRAVED

Long ago and far away, there was a carefree time in United States history. It was the era of the malt shop, blue suede shoes, the drive-in movie and ponytails. It was a time when rock 'n' roll was really rock 'n' roll, and when a house in the suburbs and a two-car garage was the ultimate and cost $15,000. It was a time when everyone was young and Americans had a great love affair with the automobile. It was Camelot! It was the Fabulous Fifties!

The Romans had their chariots and European royalty had their gilded coaches, but none of these could ever surpass the great automobiles of the 1950s. For in that decade, after a long dark period of world war and shortages of goods, America celebrated its renewed youth, prosperity and vigor with its automobiles. They were vivid, these cars, and seldom forgotten in their glowing colors and gleaming chrome, seldom equaled in their speed and luxury. They were brilliantly innovative with automatic transmissions, torsion bars, powerful engines, power steering, power brakes, (the country was power mad) and air conditioning. What was more, they were fun to drive—even easy to drive!

If anything symbolizes the cars of the 1950s, it is the fin — the tailfin dripping with chrome. The cars were designed, many of them, to suggest a racy look. The best were long and sleek with sharp, clean lines. The worst were heavily chromed, garishly colored and had fins that were nothing but ugly.

They were, however, memorable for their performance, and for the real joy and pleasure they gave their owners. How many kids grew up polishing the family car and dreaming of Saturday night at the drive-in? How many hung around the local garage just to study what was under the hood? How many hours were spent arguing whether a Chevy would outrun a Ford in a drag race? That was the love affair. Those who remember still carry a torch for the cars of that time.

The cars of the 1950s: ask anyone who remembers (and some who don't). These were the stuff of dreams, they'll tell you. How did these marvels of engineering and styling come about? Perhaps it all began with Henry Ford's Model T. The little black car with its affordable (no pun intended) price tag set free the great American wanderlust—the call of the open road. Suddenly, a whole new world beckoned

One of Ford's most acclaimed designs came about in the year 1959. Shown *at right* is a 1959 Ford Custom 300, with somewhat simpler side-chrome than its upscale brothers, the Fairlane and the Galaxie.

Opposite: This view of a 1950 Ford Custom Deluxe convertible presents a convincing argument in favor of early-1950s Fords.

The convertible was offered only with a V-8, which that year was Ford's legendary 239-ci (3.9 L) 'flathead' V-8 of 100 hp.

and a generation of eager Americans joyously embraced mobility.

The little Model Ts went everywhere, from the Texas panhandle to the Great Smokies. They traveled the legendary Route 66. They traveled through Kansas dust storms. A utilitarian automobile, a workingman's vehicle–that was the Model T.

But there are always those who want more–more speed, more comfort, more style. Inventors, tinkerers, stylists, engineers–give any of them an idea and they'll improve upon it. So it was that in the 1920s, the auto industry began to develop some of the greatest cars of all time. Such cars as the Duesenberg and the Cord set the public's pulses pounding and hearts dreaming. But such cars were only for the wealthy, driven by such people as the heroes of F Scott Fitzgerald's novels. The working man had to be content with something much less.

As the 1920s faded, the Great Depression hovered over the country. Unemployment and bread lines became harsh realities. Families migrated from the somber dust bowls of Kansas and Oklahoma to California in search of a better life. They traveled the winding, unimproved roads, as always, in the faithful Model T, looking for work–any kind of work. The Depression was a black time all across the nation. Banks in 38 states were closed. (Some would never open again.) Twelve million people were unemployed. Some sold apples on the street corners. Some picked cotton at 50 cents for 100 pounds. Many went into the Civilian Conservation Corps–the CCC as it was popularly known. Workers in the CCC made a dollar a day and their board. It was also at this time that President Franklin Roosevelt, in an effort to unify the country and aid the economy, put forth a plan to improve and increase the network of highways across the country. This, of course, produced long-term

General Motors and Chrysler Corporation were also busy attracting the public.

Opposite: A sleek 1953 Pontiac Chieftain Deluxe sedan, with a 268-ci (4.3 L) 'straight eight' engine, producing 118 or 122 hp (as compensation for the efficiency difference between standard-shift and automatic transmissions).

At left: A 1956 Dodge Custom Royal convertible. A new option this year was a push-button automatic transmission. The top engine option was a 315-ci (5.2 L) V-8 of 295 hp, though tamer versions were available.

Above: Advertising art for the 1949 Chevrolet. Its 216-ci (3.5 L) six-cylinder engine, also known as the 'stovebolt six,' cranked out 90 hp. While it really didn't offer high speed and high power, it was *very* reliable.

growth in the automobile industry, and it gave thousands immediate employment. Slowly, the nation's economy grew stronger.

Then, on 7 December 1941, the Japanese bombed Pearl Harbor. Within weeks, industry was mobilized for the war effort. Huge orders were issued for tanks, planes and ships. Civilians put aside their daily lives and went to work on defense projects. Thousands of others went off to war. It was a time of doing without. Americans, who had already experienced the hardships of the Depression, were undaunted by the wartime restrictions. They managed sugar rationing, shoe rationing, gasoline and tire rationing cheerfully, firm in the belief that each small sacrifice helped the fighting men toward winning. School children saved scrap metal and bought savings stamps which would earn them defense bonds. Everyone planted victory gardens. Women went off to work in the factories, delighted to aid the defense effort and pleased for the income.

World War II was also a time when technology bloomed. Synthetic fibers, detergents, plastics, synthetic rubber all developed as wartime grew. Nylon was a new and exciting material. It had tremendous strength, but at the same time was extremely lightweight. It was used primarily for parachutes. Rubber was in critically short supply, and synthetic rubber proved stronger and more dependable.

By the time World War II was over, the nation was back on its feet. The privation of the Depression was gone. The war was over. Optimism was the spirit of the times. If you believed in happy endings, this was it, after two decades of gloom. Dwight D Eisenhower succeeded Harry Truman as president, and one of the great national projects during the Eisenhower era was the building of a network of interstate highways linking every state in the union. The project has been likened in its scope to the building of the pyramids. At the time, did anyone realize the effect this network of highways would have on the American lifestyle? No doubt, the automobile industry did.

Looking back, it's impossible not to see that the car of the 1950s was a product of the times. The country was economically flush. A whole group of people who had come through hardship were ready for the good life as exemplified by a home in the suburbs and a new car.

A new car—the cars of the 1950s were like nothing that ever came off the assembly line, before or since. They were the stuff of dreams. And the dream was possible for

Solid construction and futuristic rocket- and jet-inspired motifs were Oldsmobile hallmarks, and hinted at the advanced engineering concepts that were so potently a part of the 1950s mystique.

At right: A 1950 Oldsmobile Ninety-Eight sedan, with a 135-hp, 303-ci (4.9 L) overhead-valve engine that the company dubbed the 'Rocket V-8.'

The interior of this top-of-the-line Oldsmobile could be ordered in nylon, broadcloth or leather. Drivetrain options included General Motors' new 'Hydra-Matic' (which spelling would change with the years) transmission.

Above: An advertisement extolling the wonders of the 1951 Oldsmobile Eighty-Eight, which stood one notch lower on the prestige ladder than the Ninety-Eight.

Though Buick then had a reputation for building ponderous cars, the 1953 Skylark convertible shown *above* proves that the company's designers were capable of clean lines and sportiness as well.

Chevrolet revealed another facet of the remarkable talents of General Motors when they unveiled their 1958 series cars. After a number of 1950s classics, the 1958 Chevrolet Bel Air (a Sport Sedan version of which is shown *opposite*) provided auto buffs with yet another stylistic gem.

everyone! Glowing with chrome and colors Henry Ford never imagined, they drew fascinated crowds to the showrooms. People awaited breathlessly the model changeover, eager to see what the designers, stylists and engineers would come up with next.

The cars of the 1950s did, indeed, reflect a kind of national exuberance. No one needed to settle for the utilitarian vehicle in this age of prosperity and optimism. However, there was more than just fins and chrome and planned obsolescence. Some of the most important automotive innovations were taking place at this time. One of the foremost was the automatic transmission, a real boon in city traffic. Critics said it lowered fuel economy, but in those times when gas was 25 cents a gallon, not too many people cared. The wraparound windshield was something new in the early 1950s car. It added a certain amount of glamour, but also gave the driver a wider range of vision.

American drivers were power mad in those days. A mild-mannered family man who got behind the wheel of the 1954 Buick Century with its 195-hp V-8 engine was suddenly transformed into a hot rod expert. Luxury and speed were what Americans wanted in their cars and it was what they got, at prices that would make today's car buyers drool! The 1956 Buick Century, for example, could go from zero to 60 mph in 10.5 seconds, exceed a speed of 110 mph and only cost about $3000.

Equally as important as speed and power was styling. No other period in automotive history has seen as much detail and concern with body shape, molding and trim. Some of the designs which came out of that period are looked on as classic— Studebaker's Loewy coupes are an example. These cars were designed, not by Raymond Loewy, but by Robert E Bourke, who was chief of the Loewy Studios at South Bend, Indiana. He had originally

intended the design as a special show model until the Studebaker management saw it and bought the design. Its clean, European styling is still considered one of the finest automotive designs of that era.

By contrast, one of the ugliest cars may have been the 1958 Buick, with its enormous chrome grille and swooping chrome-decked tailfins. So awful was this design, that it can probably serve as the archetypical overdone, over-adorned 1950s car.

On the engineering front, innovation was in full flower during the 1950s. Chrysler evolved from an inefficient L-head ('flathead') engine to an exciting, high performance powerplant. The Chrysler Saratoga with its hemispherical combustion chamber or 'hemi' V-8 engine and shorter (125.5) wheelbase, was a frequent, and often victorious, contender at stock car races in 1951. Engineering, in this era, was Chrysler's strong point. The hemi, as it developed in cars like the Chrysler New Yorker, became famous among stock car and drag racers. With modifications, it was possible to get as much as 1000 hp from this efficient engine.

Along with its engineering, the Chrysler evolved from the boxy look of the early 1950s to the sleek designs of Virgil M Exner. Exner came to Chrysler from Studebaker. His taste ran toward classic European styling. Chrysler had already pioneered with the first hardtops shortly before the 1950s, but cars produced in those early years were plain and downright unexciting. Exner's cars were based on a Ghia-bodied show car he'd first designed in 1951. Putting talent and innovation to work, he came up with the most attractive tailfins of the age. The 1957 Chrysler 300C was perhaps the best of the lot. The grille conservatively elegant, the fins clean and graceful, this was the car in which design and engineering reached a pinnacle. For though the 300C was a big, hairy-chested brute with enormous power, it was also safe, controllable–and beautiful.

An excellent, utilitarian car that received a major face-lift in the 1950s was the Chevrolet. Chevy, like Ford, had been a household word in automobiles for some 60 years. Dependable, yes. Ordinary, yes. Staid, yes. Exciting, no. But the 1950s came and things began to happen. Chevy still made ordinary family cars, because there is always a good market for ordinary family cars. However, in addition, excitement was embodied in the production of a lively little sports car called the Corvette. The Corvette first appeared in 1953 as a fiberglass two-seater that sold

for $3500. Unlike its Chevy forebears which had operated with an engine known popularly as the 'stovebolt six,' the Corvette sported a modified six-cylinder engine which delivered 150 hp. Sports car fans, however, found it hard to reconcile themselves to the automatic transmission, despite increased horsepower.

Now, what to do about 'old utility?' It was clear, because of what was going on in the rest of the industry, that Chevrolet needed a better engine, so in 1953, the familiar Chevy six was revamped and given a higher compression ratio and a displacement of 235.5-ci (3.8 L) and up to 115 hp. (Compared with the 92 hp of the old six, this was an improvement.) There it was–a steady, reliable engine, but it didn't exactly burn up the road. It took two engineers, Ed Cole and Harry Barr, to come up with something exciting. The two were always dreaming about how they'd design an engine. When the chance came in 1955, their design proved to be a milestone in automotive engines. With a displacement of 265-ci (4.4 L), the new V-8 weighed even less than the Chevy six. Short

Opposite: A sparkling front-end view of a **1958 Buick Century convertible. This was typical of the massive designs that the Buick company was known for.**

The engine was a 300 hp, 364-ci (5.9 L) overhead valve V-8. While this car appears to weigh 5000 pounds, it actually 'only' weighs 4234 pounds.

Chrysler Corporation, however, began dowdily in the early 1950s, progressing through memorable mid-decade designs to the radical look of decade's end.

Above: A 1953 Chrysler New Yorker. The **'V' on the hood signified that this car housed the early, 331-ci (5.4 L), 180-hp version of the legendary hemispherical combustion chamber ('hemi') V-8, which would come to dominate American motorsports.**

At right: Promotional artwork of a 1954 Chevrolet Bel Air sedan. The wraparound turn signal housings in the grille were an improvement over the smaller units used on the 1953 models. However, the real styling breakthrough for Chevrolet would come in 1955.

Opposite: A 1955 Chevrolet Bel Air two-door sedan. This particular car was the 50-millionth Chevrolet produced, and was dubbed 'The Golden Bel Air.'

The styling that Chevrolet presented to the car-buying public in 1955 was hailed as a classic—whether coupe, sedan, station wagon or convertible. *Above:* A 1955 Chevrolet advertisement.

This simple, appealing styling made the 1955 Chevrolet one of the most popular cars of the decade.

connecting rods additionally allowed higher rpm. Other innovations were diecast heads with integral, interchangeable valve guides, aluminum slipper pistons, and a forged, pressed steel crankshaft. Cole and Barr had been so confident of their design that they had released the engine for tooling direct from the drawing boards—a multimillion dollar gamble! As it turned out, their confidence in the design was not misplaced. The engine turned out 162 hp at 4400 rpm or 180 hp at 4600 rpm—with what Chevy called its POWERPAK. The POWERPAK was a four-barrel carburetor and dual exhausts, which gave the engine its particular throaty roar, much admired by amateur speed and performance enthusiasts.

Styling was the next consideration in the transformation of the once prosaic car. Harley Earl was chief designer at Chevrolet at that time. His guideline was 'Go all the way and then back off.' Earl liked the egg-crate grille, part of the 1953 design; the public did not. Later versions featured broader, more conventional lines. Of the Earl design team, Carl Renner was responsible for the unusual hardtop station wagon, known as the Bel Air Nomad. It was probably the most beautiful station wagon ever designed. The first of the Nomads came out in 1955, but the public found the two-door station wagons to be somewhat impractical and inconvenient.

It's sometimes interesting to know how automotive styles come about. In the early 1950s, Ford cars were characterized by a distinctive grille called the 'spinner nose.' The design came in a roundabout way from Studebaker! Styling for the Ford had been open to many designers. One of those designers was Dick Caleal, whose friends, Robert Bourke and Holden Koto, were part of the Studebaker

In 1951, Ford made trim changes on the body they'd used since 1949, and redesigned the instrument panel. For power, the 1951 models still used either a 226-ci (3.7 L) six cylinder, or the 239-ci (3.9 L) V-8 that had been earning Ford its 'hot rod' reputation since before World War II.

Above: A 1951 Ford Custom four-door sedan.

The 1951 Ford Country Squire station wagon *at right* evidences the beautiful wood exterior trim panels that so distinguished this model's appearance.

The highest trim level Ford offered for 1951 was the Custom Deluxe. *Opposite:* A 1951 Custom Deluxe convertible.

design team. Caleal requested design suggestions from his friends. Together the three built a quarter-scale clay model in the Caleal kitchen. To Mrs Caleal's dismay, they also baked it in her oven! The design was submitted to Ford's design chief, George Walker, and accepted with almost no changes as the Ford for 1949-50.

The Ford had always been a popular car and the early 'flat head' V-8 engine was the delight of hot-rodders (and moonshiners) in the 1930s–50s. From 1951 on, Ford offered an optional two-speed 'Ford-O-Matic' transmission. Before that, the company had tried, without success, to buy Studebaker's automatic shift.

The founder of the Ford Motor Company, the conservative Henry, would probably have done a swift rotation in his tomb, could he have seen the designs his company would unveil in the 1950s. In the 1950-51 model year, Ford brought out the V-8 Crestliner. It was a very special

edition two-door vehicle, selling for a mere $1711. What made it special, however, was not its price tag, but its vivid two-tone color and padded vinyl top. The two-tone pinks and wild cerises would probably have turned Henry purple. He had been famous for a remark that people could have a Ford in any color they wanted 'so long as it's black.'

Ford's production climbed during the 1950s. In 1954, the company introduced what was billed as the 'hottest engine in the low price field.' This was an overhead valve, Y-block V-8 which could produce up to 130 hp. At the same time, they introduced ball-joint front end suspension. These two innovations served to narrow the gap in engineering that existed between America's luxury and economy cars.

There were other innovations in styling: the Crestline Skyliner hardtop, developed by interior stylist L David Ash, had a front roof section made of transparent plastic. Ford's exterior design during this period, 1954-55, was greatly influenced by Frank Hershey. There was a look of speed in the clean lines and highly chromed surfaces. It was also at this time that Ford's famous 'T-Bird' was born. The Thunderbird, a spirited two-seater personal car, was envisioned by General Manager Lewis D Crusoe. Wandering through a Paris auto show, he puzzled over the question of why Ford had never developed a sports model. The idea was handed to Frank Hershey and the first T-Bird appeared in showrooms in 1955.

Another innovation from the Ford Motor Company was the Skyliner with the retractable hardtop. This came on the market in 1957. In the first year of production, Ford sold 20,766 of these retractables, but production slowed quickly. The mechanism was complicated and expensive. The retractable roof cost $350 more than a standard convertible, which the public ultimately preferred.

The times were a heyday for stylists, engineers and designers. Some of the engineers termed their work during this period as 'blue sky' projects, meaning that the sky was almost the limit on what might be accomplished. Some of the 'blue sky' projects turned out to be notable failures. Ford's Edsel was one of these.

Some of the most successful cars of the era became extinct by the late 1950s and early 1960s, but for a few brief years, such cars were truly 'king,' and an entire industry prospered because of them. Advertisers played no small role in the rise of the 1950s cars.

The 1957 Ford Fairlane 500 Skyliner was the world's only true hardtop convertible. *Above opposite:* A 1957 Skyliner during a roof retraction.

An earlier roof innovation was featured in the 1954 Ford Crestline Skyliner. The forward half of this car's roof was glass. As may be seen in the photo *at below opposite*, front-seat passengers got more than their share of sunlight.

At left: A conventional 1953 Ford Customline sedan.

Above: Advertising art featuring a 1955 Ford Sunliner convertible, offering a choice of a six or one of two V-8 engines—all of which were designed in the overhead valve configuration Ford had adopted the year before.

CITIES, SUBURBS AND THE COUNTRY SQUIRE

'Our factory buildings and equipment, materials and processes are unapproached in the entire American automobile industry...' So began a magazine advertisement for the Columbia in 1906. Advertising in those years tended to reflect more on the manufacturer and the mechanics of the vehicle than on the buyer, as autos were still proving themselves.

A great many changes had come to the automobile industry since this pre-World War I ad was written. The 1950s saw the growth of the suburbs, the baby boom, leisure time, and prosperity. There was also the youth cult, the teenaged driver with more freedom and more money than teenagers had ever had before. There was a whole generation of Americans who had come through the hard times of the Great Depression and World War II. They felt it was time to 'live a little.' The advertising industry studied the market and wrote the script.

It was, of course, apparent that certain cars were built for certain markets. The young family in the suburbs was not going to consider a sports car as a family vehicle, and the station wagon was not exactly the car for the young single executive. There were certain mottos and phrases which had grown up in the automobile advertising: Ask the Man Who Owns One; When Better Cars are Built, Buick Will Build Them; There's a Ford in Your Future; We Aim to Take Care of Our Own. These phrases were so intimately associated with the automobile that they were like part of the name.

Advertisers, creative people that they were, saw other possibilities that would sell more cars. People, they realized, no longer bought cars just for transportation. A car was a psychological machine. It said something about the person driving it. The svelte, spunky sports car was an example. Didn't it say that here was a very macho type of man with a love of speed, adventure and risk? More subtly, didn't it also imply that he was attractive, sexy, exciting, and just a little aloof? The advertisers loved this sort of thing. The public loved it even more!

Of course, the admen rightly realized that there were plenty of men, happily married with three kids, who still had quite a yen for speed and power. Detroit was building many powerful cars at this time, cars with the windswept look of speed, with tremendous horsepower. Here they

While the Fords and Chevrolets captured the hearts of many suburbanites, the as-yet conservative Chrysler styling captured the hearts of other suburb dwellers. *At right:* A 1954 Chrysler New Yorker Town & Country station wagon.

Opposite: A vivacious-looking 1956 Ford Fairlane Sunliner convertible. Two-tone paint jobs were all the rage, and this tastefully-done example shows why.

With a six, and 272-, 292- or 312-ci (4.4, 4.7 or 5.1 L) V-8s to choose from, Ford owners could also select manual (with or without overdrive) or 'Ford-O-Matic' gearboxes.

were, smack in the face of the old double standard. What will you tell your wife when you go to test drive one of these rip-roarers? At this point, the admen played down the speed and power. Now they emphasized safety and handling ability. They pointed out luxurious upholstery, roominess and comfort. They hinted at the pleasure such a car would bring to routine chores like carpooling to Little League, downtown shopping and trips to the dentist. They suggested Saturdays at antiques shows and auctions. Of course, people bought the car, and *everyone* was very happy.

Advertisers were well tuned-in to the American Dream. That dream included wealth, glamour, leisure, youth and futuristic, experimental prototypes called 'dream cars.' Buick created a convertible dream car in 1951–the Le Sabre. Publicity for this particular car shows it on a white sandy beach beneath swaying palm trees. The top is down (naturally) and sitting on the back of the seat is a suntanned dark-haired girl, attired in a bathing suit. Surely, an ad never covered all the bases quite so well or so completely. Women, who might have found the artwork annoying, were also forced to think how delightful it would be to own such a car, to drive down the highway looking wind-blown, carefree, tanned and beautiful. To them the ad said, 'Buy a Buick and you'll be lovely.'

To the men, it said many other things. It was like a kind of Siren Song. The words sang of getting away to a private Shangri-la, of long days in the warm sun frolicking on the beach in some distant, idyllic, future. None of this was probably going to happen, but the car made it seem as though at any moment it might–plus, the sense of freedom, open air, sunlight and youth was all part of the convertible mystique. No matter that you were only driving to the corner grocery to pick up a quart of milk. The convertible made it seem you were bound on some exciting rendezvous. If only Walter Mitty had owned such a convertible.

There were others whom the advertisers noticed. They had other dreams. The young American family on the way up dreamed of a home in the country, four kids and a big dog–maybe even a stable! They needed a car for their kind of lifestyle. After all, there would be ballet lessons, gymnastics, swimming meets, the orthodontist, the pediatrician, summer camp, skating lessons and riding lessons. They needed a car–even two cars! These were people who had come through the austerity of the Depression,

Opposite: The Le Sabre, a 1951 Buick 'dream car' designed by the head of GM styling, Harley Earle. Dream cars were speculative designs built and displayed to test public acceptance of various innovations. This one was powered by a supercharged 315-hp, 215-ci (3.5 L) aluminum V-8.

Above: A 1957 Ford Fairlane 500 Sunliner convertible. Note the gold, anodized aluminum side-trim panel. Power plants ranged from a six cylinder to a 300-hp, 312 ci (5.1 L) V-8.

At left: A 1952 Ford Customline sedan. While not quite a convertible, its two-tone paint job gave it an air of sportiness.

Station wagons were especially suited to that 'decade of suburbia,' the 1950s.

Above: A 1959 Ford station wagon of the Country Sedan line, which was a companion to Ford's Ranch Wagon and Country Squire station wagon lines that year.

Ford offered its station wagons in either six-cylinder or V-8 variants with two- and four-door configurations of six- or nine-passenger capacity.

people who had said, 'My child is going to have all the advantages I never had.'

The advertisers embroidered on the Dream. They pictured sleek station wagons drawn up in front of posh country clubs. Or they showed the kids and the family dog, cute as could be, piled into a roomy nine-passenger, about to embark for Grandma's. They showed wonderful, wood-sided station wagons parked outside elegant country estates. There was an aura here of landed gentry, private schools, and blueblood connections. And though for most people it wasn't true-to-life, still there was the element of possibility.

The station wagon also said things about the people who drove it. A man behind the wheel of a station wagon was probably a family man who played golf on Saturdays, maybe went out hunting and fishing with a couple of good buddies and probably took his family camping in the summer. An ad for a 1959 Dodge Sierra station wagon shows three enthusiastic sportsmen heading out for bird hunting amid glorious fall foliage. One can almost feel the nip in the air! And what a lot of gear you could stow in that practical rear storage area.

Change the scene now and here are the ladies about to take the same wagon. They're the typical suburban matrons, beautifully groomed and nicely dressed. They would be off to a bridge luncheon or to play tennis at the club. Or they might be bound to the city to visit the art galleries, do some shopping and meet their husbands for dinner. A station wagon was certainly a social vehicle, offering, as it did, such a lot of room.

The 1950s were the years of the 'Baby Boom.' The station wagon came into its own in these years. How else could you haul nine Little League players and all that equipment to the championship game? How else could you car pool six kids to elementary school? It was the only way to get Roxy and her litter to the vet's for their shots. Suburban mothers, who spent so much time on the road, cherished their 'wagons' almost as much as their favorite hair-dressers. There were, as mentioned, the fun trips, too. You could pick a bargain at a country auction and bring it home easily in the accommodating wagon. You could put all the skis on the roof rack and be off for the slopes in a jiffy. You could cart home a bushel of apples, two huge pumpkins and a gallon of cider from one of those quaint little country stands. And, best of all, the wonderful roominess of the wagon put distance between you and the kids and the dog! Ah, sweet oblivion!

The all-American automobile had evolved at this point into something more than just a vehicle. A lot of the appeal of certain models was as much psychological as anything else. Did anyone really need all that power, all that speed, all that chrome? Probably not. But it felt good and it looked good. Such sensuousness was irresistible to many. The Dodge was a case in point. In the early 1950s, Dodge had been a very ho-hum automobile with the usual six-cylinder engine and what was described as 'three-box' styling. In 1953, however, Dodge emerged as something far, far different from the stodgy car it had been.

As a division of Chrysler Corporation, Dodge fell heir to the hemi-head engine that Chrysler engineers had long been perfecting. The Dodge engine that year was a some-what scaled down version of Chrysler's 331 (5.4 L). Called the Red Ram V-8, the engine offered 140 hp plus. Further improved by Virgil Exner's styling, the Dodge took wings as a performance car. That year a Dodge V-8 won the Mobilgas Economy Run and broke nearly 200 records at the land speed trials at Bonneville, Utah. Such records boosted the sales of Dodge enormously. One could point to the gasoline economy (Dodge V-8 got 23.4 mpg) and

Above: A 1959 DeSoto Firesweep station wagon. The Firesweep designation was the lowest DeSoto trim line for that year. The standard power plant was a 361-ci (5.9 L) V-8, mated to either a three-speed standard or one of Chrysler Corporation's renowned Torqueflite automatics.

At left: One of the reasons the station wagon as a type became so popular. This 1954 Ford Crestline Country Squire had simplicity of line and balance of detail. This design added considerable pleasure to driving such a basically utilitarian vehicle.

say what a good 'common sense' investment such a car was, but on the other hand, all that speed, power and grace didn't dampen enthusiasm, either. Behind the wheel of a Dodge, one could envision the long, salt flats of Bonneville, the sting of alkali and the exhilarating speed.

A fantasy, yes, but it lifted one out of the ordinary daily grind just to slip behind the wheel of such a car.

No one is immune to such fantasies. Nearly every car on the market was undergoing the same metamorphosis as Dodge. American tastes had grown more sophisticated and demanding. At the same time though, owning a car had become a necessity. Previous to the 1950s, railroads handled most commuter and long-haul passengers. However, the equipment toll taken by extra-heavy World War II traffic, plus increasing long-distance airline service, and certainly not least of all, heavily-patronized pro-automobile legislation dealt severe blows to the railroads. The car and the bus were 'local' rivals. The car was the link between home in the suburbs and the job in the city, the doctor's

Manufacturers did their best to appeal to as wide a range of tastes as possible. This was especially true of the large, heavy convertibles of the 1950s.

They looked flashy, but had a substantiality that was appealing to the family sensibility.

Above: A 1952 Cadillac Series 62 convertible. With a 331-ci (5.4 L) V-8 under its hood, this car offered both luxury and a highbrow kind of sportiness.

Opposite: A 1955 Pontiac Star Chief convertible. The base engine for all Pontiacs this year was a 287-ci (4.7 L) V-8. A performance kit was optionally available.

While the 1956 Ford Country Squire station wagon shown *at right* stands in contrast to the convertibles, it was an even more popular car.

Chrysler Corporation was one of many late-1950s carmakers that featured tailfins in their designs.

Plymouths, Dodges, DeSotos and Chryslers were all graced with such jet-age-inspired appendages.

Below: A 1959 Plymouth Sport Fury convertible. An option was the 305-hp, 360-ci 'Golden Commando' V-8. This was a car that had power to go with its attention-getting looks.

Opposite: A beautifully-styled 1955 Plymouth Belvedere. Note the nascent tailfins. The next year, these would become prominent.

office, the school and downtown shopping. Because so much depended on getting to these places, Americans demanded reliability from their automobiles. Tailfins or no, nothing could be worse than being stuck in city traffic with an engine that just conked out—well, it could be worse if you had the kids and Rover.

This was a time, however, when automotive engineering had made tremendous strides. Not only were automobiles more powerful than they had ever been, they often were extremely reliable. True, there were occasional 'lemons,' but these were due more to production line flukes than to engineering defects. The manufacturers issued with each new car an owner's manual with specific maintenance instructions. This wasn't exactly a new idea, but with the newer engines it was a necessity. The owner's manual was required reading, listing oil changes, types of oil to use, tire rotation, times for engine tune-ups and the details to be checked at each tune-up. Toward the end of the 1950s, some car companies, such as Chrysler, developed a warranty against engine defects. Chrysler, whose motto was,

'We aim to take care of our own' was known for its outstanding engineering.

Chrysler owners were encouraged to take their cars back to the dealer for service and parts rather than going to the local gas station. This kind of service earned consumer loyalty, kept people coming into the showroom 'just to look' at newer models and also increased business for the dealer. Most car dealers had picked up on the service angle. It was a very logical outgrowth of sales. If you sold it, why not service it? It was also part of the reliability factor. A local mechanic who saw a car on a regular basis got to 'know' it and its owner very well. The busy suburban family relied on the mechanic for their car problems as much as they relied on their pediatrician for the children's ills. Service became a consideration in the sale of a car.

That the American lifestyle was changing sharply in this decade was apparent. That the automobile had influenced this change was also apparent. The burgeoning middle class, the new prosperity, the network of fine highways that spread across the country and, in no small way, the great American Dream, had changed the country more dramatically than anyone would ever have guessed.

Opposite: A 1959 Plymouth Fury four-door sedan. Obviously, that year's Plymouths were designed to look long, low and futuristic. The standard Plymouth V-8 was a 318-ci (5.2 L) engine that proved to be extremely reliable.

At left: A 1955 Pontiac Chieftain 860 Colony station wagon. This was a six-passenger vehicle, with storage room in the back, and—like most station wagons—a fold-down rear seat.

Above: A 1955 Oldsmobile Super Eighty-Eight Holiday sedan. The 'Super' appellation refers to the use in otherwise lower-level Eighty-Eight series cars of the high-power engine previously used only in the upper-level Ninety-Eight series cars.

POWER STEERING, THE AUTOMATIC TRANSMISSION AND WOMEN

The American lifestyle had changed. In the 1930s and 1940s, the city had been the place to live. There was the convenience of public transportation, neighborhood shopping, and the close proximity of theaters, galleries and museums. Cities in those years seemed to offer all the advantages of the good life. But Americans of the 1950s yearned for space, fresh air, wholesome country living and the small towns that spoke of an easier, slower way of life. The country or a small town, that was the place to raise children. Many cities were slowly falling into decay. They were dirty and crowded, their neighborhoods had changed, crime was growing and they had ceased embodying America's dreams.

There was also a tremendous building boom going on. Young veterans of both World War II and the Korean Conflict needed homes for their families. Suburban houses sprouted like mushrooms. Row upon row upon row of neat little look-alike homes sprang up on streets with names like Shady Lane (no trees, of course), or Wendy's Way. Although these emerging suburbs looked very sterile, it didn't matter to the proud new homeowners. In fact, people made jokes about walking into the wrong house because they all looked so much alike, or that they all had been produced by a giant cookie cutter. What often made these suburban neighborhoods different from their counterparts in the city or small towns, however, was the lack of an easily accessible village center of shops, churches, schools and other services.

In their exodus to the country, the families of the 1950s had left behind all the services the cities provided. It was no longer an easy two-block walk to the grocery store but a 15-mile pilgrimage twice a week. And it was a five-mile run to the nearest school. Luckily, there were a lot of children, so carpools could be arranged. The car was in daily use, and it was Mom who did the chauffeuring. Other changes occurred because of this suburban growth: traffic swelled, roads were improved, and cars became easier and safer to drive.

The automatic transmission first appeared in the late 1940s. Consumers eyed it cautiously. Sports car types who preferred the more efficient manual transmissions openly sneered and continued to shift for themselves. But Moms loved it. Driving as they did, in all kinds of traffic, the automatic shift was a joy. There was no longer any of the

Opposite: **Oh! The joy of owning a nice, new shiny 1959 Edsel Corsair! Conceived in the mid-1950s to fill the gap between Ford's lower- and higher-priced offerings, the Edsel series debuted in 1957 — the year the market for medium-priced cars bottomed out.**

constant shifting from high to low to second. With an automatic shift, one could pay more attention to traffic and to finding a place to park!

That was another problem–finding a place to park. One had to drive into the city to shop, along with a million other people. Traffic was horrible, parking was nearly impossible and the whole ordeal threatened your sanity. But then, on cue, came a wonderful innovation. Far from the maddening crowd, with acres of parking space and lots and lots of shops, came the shopping mall. It was a godsend to the suburban dweller. You still had to drive to the mall, but there was less traffic and you could always find a parking spot. Malls would take over a decade catching on.

Americans at this time were developing a taste for luxury. The house on Wendy's Way had wall-to-wall carpets and the new den had floor-to-ceiling oak paneling. There was also a downstairs powder room. How did anyone manage with just one bathroom before? And there was a 'rec' room in the basement with a TV and a bar and a stereophonic phonograph. In the beginning, such things

were considered 'extras,' but then such luxuries became necessities. Soon, no one thought twice about building a house with two and one-half baths, and wall-to-wall carpeting was de rigueur.

This growing appetite for luxury was also reflected in the family car. Carpeting and upholstery were just as elegant as in the living room at home. New automobiles sprouted numerous small conveniences. Many were standard equipment; others were optional. Cigar lighters, tinted glass, map lights, arm rests, bucket seats and air conditioners were added. Packard did away with the cluttered 'glove compartment' and offered a drawer instead. Although it was highly practical, no other car ever adopted the idea. Air conditioning was a real boon to the motorist. It offered a cool, pleasant ride on even the hottest day. It also offered peace from traffic noise, since the windows had to be rolled up when the unit was operating. Bucket seats also found a ready market in the tall man/short lady combination. Mom could drive Dad to the train station without him having to sit with his knees up by his ears!

Below: A 1958 Bonneville Custom convertible. Such cars exemplified the idea of combining sporty styling with luxurious size. Note the 'rocket' motif just behind the front door.

Opposite: Another example of the 1958 Custom convertible—with one of several special interiors offered by the company. This car's extravagant flair underscores the fact that General Motors stylists could cope with almost any customer's sense of taste.

On this and the following pages

Cadillac

proudly presents

A NEW AMERICAN CLASSIC!

At left: A 1958 Fleetwood Sixty Special four-door hardtop model, with Detroit, Michigan in the background. Cadillac represented the ultimate in American luxury, with such makes as Lincoln's Continental and Chrysler's Imperial offering tough competition.

The factory base price in 1958 for a brand-new Sixty Special hardtop was $6232.

Above: A magazine advertisement for Cadillac's 1958 models, touting Fleetwood styling and the famous Cadillac air-bag suspension.

Above: A 1957 Eldorado Brougham four-door hardtop. This car was derived from the designs of early-1950s Cadillac 'dream cars' (see also caption, page 25). This car was loaded with standard items, including an Arpège atomizer loaded with Lanvin perfume.

Power was provided by a 325-hp, 365-ci (5.9 L) V-8. Narrow whitewalls on the tires—in contrast to then-common wide whitewalls—were standard.

The luxury car of luxury cars has always been the Cadillac. So it was in the 1950s, and so it will probably always be. The Cadillac of the early 1950s was one of the best road cars of that time. Cadillacs were expensive, but justifiably so, with their custom interiors and panoramic windshields. Long known as the 'Standard of the World,' the Cadillac of the 1950s was truly an elegant car. The Cadillac Eldorado was a limited edition in 1953. Only 532 were built that year. Priced at $7750, they were the most expensive cars sold that year. The Eldorado convertible was one of the most luxurious Cadillacs ever. A special metal boot covered the folded down convertible top. The interior styling, all of it custom, was exquisite.

In 1957, Cadillac introduced the Eldorado Brougham, a very expensive ($13,000) and very unusual car. The Brougham featured a brushed aluminum roof, quadruple head lights and the distinctive styling by Ed Glowacke. The Brougham was a pillarless sedan. Looking like a very regal 'hard top' with doors that opened in the center, it was also equipped with air suspension. Air suspension had been around since 1952, but it had never been used on a passenger car before. It provided, or was supposed to provide, a very smooth, level ride, but because the cost and maintenance of air suspension was so high, Cadillac soon dropped this system.

The Chrysler was another of the luxury cars of the 1950s.

It was not quite in the same class as the Cadillac, but still a fine car known for excellent engineering and handling ease. In 1953, Chrysler had introduced a two-speed automatic transmission known as Powerflite. Powerflite had evolved into a three-speed transmission called Torqueflite by 1957. Torqueflite was one of the finest automatic transmissions ever built. Chrysler also developed the Torsionaire ride. This consisted of torsion bars on the front wheels to eliminate road shock. Torsion bars were a major contribution to good handling.

The Lincoln had always been known as a luxurious but sedate automobile. In the 1950s it began a slow transformation. The first new development was the V-8 valve-in-head engine capable of 160 hp when first introduced in 1952. It boasted such innovations as oversized intake valves, which allowed for greater efficiency and output per cubic inch of engine size. There were eight counterweights on the crankshaft instead of the usual six, making it one of the smoothest-running engines ever. By the time the 1953 models were on the market, this engine could produce 205 hp with greater efficiency than either Cadillac or Chrysler.

Starting in 1952, Lincolns were also equipped with ball-joint front suspension. The ball-joint suspension proved to be a very controllable, flexible system. Further improvements were recirculating ball power steering, sound-

Above: A 1967 Cadillac Series 62 convertible. Series 62 Cadillacs were the lowest level offered by America's premier luxury carmaker that year. They were also the smallest. Even so, this Series 62 convertible was indeed luxuriant enough for almost anybody, and had a factory base price of $5225, at a time in which a Ford Sunliner convertible cost $2505.

deadening insulation and oversized drum brakes, plus an optional four-way power seat. There was also optional factory air conditioning with flow-through ventilation. The interior, with its fine quality fabric and leathers, reflected the ultimate in quiet, elegant taste.

The Kaiser was an interesting luxury car. The 1951 model prompted a good deal of enthusiasm. It offered more glass, ease of handling and some of the most unique styling of the 1950s. Most luxurious of all was the 1953 Kaiser hardtop Dragon sedan. The Dragon sported gold-plated exterior trim plus a padded top. Inside, the car was upholstered in a fabric called 'Laguna' cloth, created by fashion designer Marie Nichols. The Dragon had everything: tinted glass, Hydra-Matic drive, white-wall tires, a dual speaker radio and special custom carpeting on the floor and inside the trunk. There was a gold medallion on the dash which could be engraved with the owner's name. All of these features were standard accoutrements on the Dragon. But such a spectacular car demanded an equally spectacular price. The Dragon's $3320 tag did not make it

Mercury was one notch above Ford in the hierarchy of Ford Motor Company lines.

Above: A 1953 Mercury Sport Coupe. Power windows, power steering and power brakes were options, but most importantly, it was a great car for families on the rise.

Contrasted to the overtly sporty lines of the Mercury just previously discussed, the popular 1951 DeSoto Custom coupe shown *at right* is simply well-proportioned, and rather cute.

Lincoln, Ford's luxury car line, produced two main models in 1956—the Lincoln proper (which included the Capri and Premier subseries), and the Continental (see pages 92–95), which was another kind of luxury car altogether.

Opposite: A 1956 Lincoln Premier. This car won design awards for its many built-in safety features, including improved door locks and deep-dish steering wheel.

Cadillac was number one, Lincoln was number two and Chrysler's Imperial was number three in prestige among America's luxury car lines.

Below: A 1956 Imperial. Chrysler Corporation liked such unusual styling touches as perching the taillights atop the rear fins, as is seen here.

When it came to giving the impression of length, lowness and sheer expanse of fin area, few manufacturers could compete with Chrysler Corporation.

Opposite: A 1957 Chrysler Imperial hardtop. Note the unusual 'overlapping' design of the rear roof section.

especially popular with the public. Only 1277 Dragons were ever built.

The Imperial, an outgrowth of Chrysler's top line, became a separate make of automobile in 1955. It was totally a luxury car, with the same sort of quiet taste seen in Cadillac and Lincoln. The Imperial was powered by a 331-ci (5.4 L) V-8 engine, of the famous 'hemi' configuration, which produced 250 hp. In 1956, the new models featured a bored-out version of the same engine, 354-ci (5.8 L), and were capable of 280 hp. Powerflite transmission on the Imperial was standard. The only special option was air conditioning. By 1957, the Imperial had evolved the huge tailfins so typical of Virgil Exner's 'Forward' look. These came standard with the Torqueflite three-speed transmission and a formidable 392 (6.4 L) hemi-head engine, which produced 325 hp. The Imperial was an arresting, exciting sight, and it outsold Lincoln for the first time ever. Dealers were consistently frustrated by people who still referred to the car as the Chrysler Imperial. Chrysler, while a fine car, never carried the prestige that Cadillac (Imperial's rival) did.

Packard was a grand old name in luxury cars. Before the Great Depression, Packard had been famous for its taste-

ful and expensive automobiles. But the company would have died in the 1930s had it not brought out a line of lower-priced cars. When the automobile companies began building again in 1945, Packard offered its basic pre-war design again (as did nearly all the auto manufacturers). Then, a 1948 update on this design was unveiled, and was known by many as the 'pregnant elephant' which was, unfortunately, an apt description of the car.

Style, however, did not interfere with the roadability of the Packard. The Packard was beautifully engineered, smooth and powerful on the road. The 'pregnant elephant'

was entirely redesigned for 1951 by John Reinhart. Packard, unfortunately, clung to its lower-priced line while at the same time it brought out the more traditional Packard. Among these more traditional types was the Mayfair, which came out in both a hardtop and a convertible. The Mayfair was elegantly trimmed, a lively, sporty car which appealed to buyers.

Packard was limping along when James Nance became president of the company in 1952. The plant was working at 50 percent of capacity when he took over. Nance relegated the inexpensive line to a separate make called the Clipper, and Packard went back to building luxury cars. The Patrician was the top of the Packard line, a formal car with a leather top and tiny rear windows, priced at $6531 in 1953. In the same year, Packard introduced a glamorous convertible called the Caribbean as a limited edition. The Caribbean, with its 180 hp engine, was well received and outsold Cadillac's Eldorado that year.

The Hudson in the 1950s was a marginal luxury car. It was a large unit body automobile which one stepped down into, a car that seemed to place emphasis on comfort and aerodynamics. The Hudson Hornet won fame as a spunky

CUSTOM CONSTELLATION
245 HORSEPOWER

Head of its Class in Everything...

in QUALITY . . . "Built by Packard Craftsmen"
means that the Clipper is the only medium-priced
car with a fine car background. Dramatically designed,
efficiently engineered, everything about the Clipper
bespeaks quality.

in SIZE . . . nearly 18 impressive feet of exterior
beauty surrounds luxuriously large interiors . . .
uncramped, uncrowded space for heads and shoulders,
hips and legs . . . the room you need to ride relaxed.

in POWER . . . highest power rating in the medium-

price field with two brilliant V-8 engines developing
245 and 225 horsepower. Delivering this tremendous
driving force to the rear wheels is the new Twin
Ultramatic, smoothest and most responsive of all
automatic transmissions.

The individually distinctive Clipper offers most
Quality, Size and Power . . . most car for your
money in the medium-price field.

You are invited to drive the Clipper, product of
Packard Division, Studebaker-Packard Corporation.

Visit Your Clipper Dealer Today . . . Take the Key and See

for those who desire individuality... the 1955 *Clipper* *Built by Packard Craftsmen*

CUSTOM FOUR DOOR
245 HORSEPOWER

contender in the NASCAR races. The Jet Liner series, Hudson's luxury line, sparked a sort of American-Italian marriage, which culminated in the exciting looking Italia. The Italia was a four-passenger *gran turismo* designed by Frank Spring, Hudson's chief designer, and built by the Carrozzeria Touring Company of Milan.

The Italia was as Italian as the standard Hudson was not. It had elegance and styling, wraparound windshield, doors which were cut into the roofline, functional airscoops, leather seats and flow through ventilation. But Hudson's finances were shaky. There was not enough money for a firm commitment to this car, so only 25 plus the prototype and a single four-door model–called the X161– were ever produced, which were sold at $4800 each. They were Hudson's last attempt at a luxury car. In 1955, Hudson and Nash merged, and Hudson faded.

The American family, as part of its taste for luxury, now often owned two cars. Two cars, in fact, were often a necessity. Dad, who commuted to work in the city, needed a car to get him at least as far as the Park and Ride lot at the train station. Mom, at home with all the burgeoning family responsibilities, also relied on the car to handle the myriad errands which she faced. For a while, they managed nicely with one car. Mom merely scheduled all the errands for one particular day. On that day she drove Dad to the train station and the car was hers. But there were numerous times when two cars would ease the conflict, so families often succumbed and bought a station wagon, which became Mom's car, and a regular sedan, which Dad used to drive to work.

No one thought much about the inefficiencies of such a situation. Driving a full-sized car with a powerful engine in city traffic or leaving it parked in a parking lot all day was what everyone did. There was really not much choice in the matter, because no one had yet thought of a commuter car.

No one, that is, except George Mason of Nash. Contrary to every other manufacturer of the times, George Mason loved little cars. The Nash Rambler was his 'baby,' so to speak. The Big Three auto manufacturers had not thought much about the compact car, but George Mason, with great foresight, saw the value of the small car, particularly since none of the other companies had such a model. The Rambler came out in the early 1950s as a two-door station wagon and an unusual landau convertible. This convertible, unlike any other, had permanently fixed window frames. Only the roof folded down. In 1951, a hardtop was added to the line. But the top seller for Rambler was the practical and attractive wagon. It was an ideal suburban car. In fact, 22 percent of the station wagons sold at that time were Ramblers. For a small automobile company, this was a huge success.

It hardly needs to be mentioned that more and more women began to drive in the 1950s. Time was when driving had been the prerogative of the man of the house, but by the 1950s, women had taken over the wheel, and they loved it. Car manufacturers were beginning to realize what dealers had known all long: that an automobile had to appeal to the wife as well as the husband. Dodge went so far as to manufacture a dream car called *La Femme*, a

Custom Royal Lancer two-door hardtop. It featured a pink exterior and white upholstery. Other little custom accoutrements were a folding umbrella and a handbag designed to rest in the backs of the front seats. The pink and white car caused a real stir at automotive shows in 1955 and 1956. The interest seemed strong enough to send the car into serious production, but Dodge decided against it. Only a few of these cars were ever produced.

For the American woman, the car was one of the great liberating forces of her life. It gave her the freedom and the ability to travel anywhere she pleased with ease and comfort that had never existed before. There was security in the big, powerful, reliable cars, and there was real pleasure and exhilaration in driving them.

Packard had been one of the hallowed names in American luxury cars up until the latter years of the Great Depression, when a slump in the luxury car market was the beginning of decline for the independent company—while such as Cadillac stayed afloat on the finances of their parent companies.

As of the mid-1950s, Packard was a company teetering on collapse. Packard offered a medium-price car, the Clipper, and upper-level cars including the Packard proper and the Caribbean subseries, with such options as reversible leather/brocade upholstery.

Opposite: An advertisement for the 1955 Packard Clipper. Packard merged with Studebaker on 2 June 1954.

Economy was a facet of the 1950s American automotive scene that Nash Motors cashed in on at the outset of the decade.

At left: Members of an increasingly automotive American populace pass by each other in their 1952 Nash Rambler Country Club two-door hardtop coupes.

Small enough to fit into two-thirds of the average parking space, and economical with an 82-hp six-cylinder engine, the Nash Rambler line was highly popular, especially in station wagon form.

WHITE BUCKS AND SADDLE SHOES

*T*wo things did more to put American teenagers on wheels in the 1950s than anything else. One was the ready availability of jobs in those years and the other was the auto manufacturer's policy of 'planned obsolescence.' Teenagers of the 1950s, for the first time in history, had money to spend, more money than any teenage generation before. Like their elders, they were intrigued with cars. They spent their Saturdays and their free time looking at cars, working on cars, talking cars, going to and participating in 'drag races.' Owning a car then, as now, was a special badge of maturity and freedom. And if you owned the 'right' car, you would have to beat the girls (or boys) off with a stick!

Planned obsolescence was a kind of scheme that worked because the automobile companies were riding the tide of a seller's market. Nearly every year, when the new models came out, there would be changes in the cars. Every two to three years there would be a dramatic styling change, and yearly, there would be engineering changes. Sometimes there would be only minor engine innovations, but even so, last year's car was just not as up-to-date or glamorous as the newest model. So, many people changed cars every two or three years. The old models were far from worn out. Many, in fact, were just nicely broken in, and this was where the teenage market came in.

For a little money, one could go down to Easy Harry's Used Car Lot and make a heck of a deal on a 1954 Dodge or a 1953 Chevy. 'A beautiful car,' Harry would say, 'not a scratch on it. Purrs like a kitten. Sure, try it out.'

The funny thing was that this car, was all that Harry said it was. Of course, with a little work, it would blow everybody away at the drag strip! That was part of the fun of owning a car—just seeing how much power you might get from that engine by applying the right kind of speed equipment.

The Ford flathead V-8 was a prime target for the hot-rodder. Straight from the factory, with no modifications, the V-8 could churn out 110 hp at 3800 rpm. Chrysler Corporation, with its much coveted hemi-head engine, became one of the all-time delights of the hot-rod crowd. Its engine, with minor modifications to exhaust, carburetors, and camshaft, might achieve 400 hp. Drag racers who really worked on the engine and added a supercharger could get as much as 1000 hp from the hemi.

But such work was costly and complicated. To begin

The hardtop was great type of car for a 1950s teenager to borrow from Mom and Dad in order to impress friends. With no side pillars, the roof seemed like a canopy for a triumphal procession.

At right: A 1953 Ford Crestline Victoria hardtop with windows down.

Opposite: A 1954 Corvette. This was also impressive, if you could get Dad to loan you his (which was doubtful). It was 'just for looks,' however, as this little car's 150-hp six cylinder engine was mismatched with a low-performance automatic transmission.

with, the hemi, with its massive engine block, was heavy and expensive. Modifying it required special heads, a radical camshaft, new intake and exhaust manifolds and other expensive goodies. It also took time and money to achieve all the power the hemi was capable of delivering. A lot of kids had to be satisfied with the dream, and for many that was enough. Parents and the local police tended to view such vehicles with a very critical eye.

When Chevrolet came out with its V-8 in 1955, it also became another car to delight teenagers. The lightweight 265 (4.4 L) could deliver 162 hp at 4400 rpm. Its short "stroke" helped to boost the rpm. It was a great car for the drag strip even though its torque was low.

The real dream cars of those years, however, were Ford's snazzy Thunderbird (the two-seater model) and Chevy's Corvette. Anyone who was lucky, a born salesman, or possessed of an innocent parent might con his family into buying such a car 'for commuting.' The next thing was to

Chevrolet's design for the 1955–56 model years attracted everyone, including hot rodders, who tended to do only minor cus-tomizing on the *classic* body itself, preferring to add performance parts to the engine and drivetrain (or to simply give the car entirely new running gear), even though the stock 265-ci (4.4 L) V-8, when equipped with Chevrolet's 'POWERPAK' option, produced 180 hp.

Magnesium-alloy, or 'mag,' wheels are a present-day tag for spotting souped-up 1955–56 Chevrolets. In the 1950s, how-ever, they simply chromed the stock wheels or fitted them with custom hub-caps for a sense of individuality.

The upper-level Bel Air was preferred. *Opposite:* A 1955 Chevrolet Bel Air sedan, with mag wheels.

Above: A close-up of a 1955 Chevrolet Bel Air with a non-stock blacked-in grille.

At left: A candy-apple red and white 1956 Chevrolet Bel Air sedan with mag wheels. Similar cars helped to establish Chevro-let's status as a favorite among the teenagers of the 1950s.

con the parents into letting you drive it! Should you, by some strange quirk of fate, accomplish these various tasks, then the world was yours. The Prom Queen ignored the football hero, every girl in the senior class was panting to go out with you and your buddies all wanted to look under the hood. There was no greater victory than to pull into the local root beer stand on a Saturday night in such a super car with two or three of the most desirable cheerleaders in tow. Ah, how sweet it was! That is, it was sweet until you were awakened the next morning by an irate father who asked why you hadn't thought to refill the gas tank.

The 'T-Bird' first came out in 1955. With its rakish looks, it became an immediate success—even a legend. Ford's overhead valve Y-block V-8 had been bored out to 292-ci (4.7 L) for the Bird. The engine was capable of producing nearly 200 hp. The first 1955 edition sold over 16,000 cars. Rock stars sang about it, dealers praised it, and fathers fumed every time the kids took it out.

At right and opposite: Two views of a 1955 Ford Thunderbird. The first year Thunderbird was strictly a convertible—the fiberglass top shown here lifted off. A fabric convertible-style top was optional.

The Thunderbird was an instant classic, with style and plenty of power. The option list for this car included power steering, power windows, power brakes and power seats.

With dual exhausts that gave off a pleasing rumble, the Thunderbird V-8 was an overhead-valve, 292-ci (4.7 L), 193-hp power plant that took the little car in conquest of records everywhere.

Above: This 1957 Thunderbird has a heavier front end than the original, and a longer rear end as well. The Thunderbird was to change a lot over the years, eventually becoming a four-seater, and getting larger in general.

Chevy's Corvette had been introduced to the public in 1953. It was America's first postwar sports car. Like the T-Bird, it was a two-seater, ideally cozy with the right person. Stylewise, it was not quite as dashing as the Thunderbird, but still nothing to be sneezed at, either. A Corvette could be equally as enticing as a T-Bird to any cheerleader. In the beginning, however, the Corvette had been considerably less powerful than the 'T.' With its modified six-cylinder engine and automatic transmission, it was capable of 150 hp. When Ford came out with the T-Bird in 1955, Chevy made a V-8 optional on the Corvette, which boosted the horsepower and kept the 'Vette' in the competition.

There were other highly-desired cars in those years. A convertible of any type was almost a sure-fire guarantee of

a red hot date for Saturday night. They were likewise more expensive, even as used cars. But every once in a while, with some judicious trading, one could acquire a 'flop top.' Nearly every manufacturer in those pre-Ralph Nader times offered a convertible. Buick brought out a limited edition sports convertible in 1953. Called the Skylark, it sported Kelsey Hayes chrome wire wheels and none of the portholes so typical of Buicks at that time. Only 1690 of this particular model were produced and they wore a price tag of $5000. Not exactly a car you could drive home to Mother, but there were many, many others, each unique and special in its own way.

Pontiac, in 1955, came out with its first V-8 engine, called the Strato-Streak. It was a spunky, if conventional, design capable of 180 hp without the optional four-barrel carbure-

Opposite: **A 1959 Corvette. Compare this with the Corvette shown on page 48. The base engine for this car was a 283-ci (4.6 L) V-8, available in variants up to a 290-hp, fuel-injected version, with a choice of a three- or a four-speed manual transmission.**

Buick brought out their limited-edition Skylark convertible for a second year in 1954. The engine was a 200-hp, 322-ci (5.2 L) V-8, mated to Buick's smooth but terribly slushy Dynaflow automatic transmission. *Below:* **A 1954 Buick Skylark convertible.**

Pages 56–57: Pontiac was a well-built but not extremely popular car. Then the company went for the 'youth market' with such as this 1956 Star Chief convertible.

The power plant was a 316-ci (5.1 L) V-8. As was Pontiac's modus operandi, cars equipped with manual transmissions were tuned to 216 hp, while cars with automatic transmissions were tuned to 227 hp.

Chevrolet managed to do with the 'fin look' what they had with the more conservative dictates of the years 1955–56 (see pages 50–51), and produced a car that was similarly popular, especially with hot rodders.

The base engine was a 283-ci (4.6 L) V-8, available in variants of from 185 to 283 hp, and mated to a variety of transmissions (though the most popular with hot rodders was the close-ratio three-speed manual unit).

Some preferred to leave the car unaltered, and others souped up the drivetrain, just as they had this 'Chevy's' immediate predecessors. *At right:* A somewhat customized 1957 Chevrolet Bel Air sedan.

The archetypal 1950s 'street rod' was the 1950 Mercury, which had felicitous lines and a 255-ci (4.1 L) V-8 engine that was as easy to build into competition form as was the legendary 239-ci (3.9 L) Ford V-8.

The favorite treatment was lowering the car, so that it appeared to glide along. Some hot rodders also smoothed out a line here and there, and others merely polished what was *already* considered to be perfection.

Opposite: A lowered 1950 Mercury two-door coupe, with custom wheels and a gleaming finish.

tor. Given the optional carburetor, it was easily capable of 200 hp. Moreover, the engine ran on regular gas and had an 8:1 compression ratio. The Star Chief convertible was a knockout in the series. It featured a wraparound windshield, tubeless white sidewall tires, and two-tone paint. It was one to set your sights on.

These were the years when the 'drive-in' was a new phenomenon. There were drive-in movies; drive-in root beer stands, with their snappy waitresses who delivered an order right to the car; and drive-in car washes, where one could get his car washed, buffed and waxed without ever leaving the driver's seat.

The car spelled freedom and kindled a quiet revolution in how the nation's youth spent their leisure time. No longer did a boy walk his girl to the movies or spend summer nights sitting in a porch swing holding hands. Now they went off to anywhere–the beach, an amusement park, downtown, uptown, the drag races and, best of all, the drive-in movie.

There were also countless hours of driving up and down main street just to see what was happening or, better yet, to be seen. There were private drag races out on dark, country roads. It was exciting, it was fun, and not even the teenagers really understood what it was all about.

Below: A 1958 Chevrolet convertible. In addition to being at the top Chevrolet trim level, the 1958 Impala carried an air of elegance, with its low, flowing lines.

Since these cars could be had with engines ranging from a 185-hp, 283-ci (4.6 L) V-8 to a 315-hp, 348-ci (5.7 L) V-8, the Impala also had a reputation for performance. The convertible model especially was a splendid 'cruising' car.

There were the Saturday nights after the movies, when no one wanted to go home yet, when everyone would gather at the local hamburger joint and drive 'round and 'round the place yelling mild insults at the fellow ahead. Sometimes it went on for an hour or more, nobody wanting to drop out.

It was a time of warm summer nights, listening to Chuck Berry, Elvis Presley and Little Richard, a time between the Korean Conflict and the protest marches of the 1960s, a time when everyone laid back and had fun. Pollution? Nobody thought of it. Energy Crisis? What was that? Gas was 30 cents a gallon. Steel shortages? Never! It was a time when people had strong ideas about right and wrong, good and bad.

TV was just coming onto the scene. Lucille Ball and Desi Arnez, Kukla, Fran and Ollie, the Honeymooners…sex

and violence? Not in the living room of the 1950s!

There was the generation gap, a boundary between adolescence and adulthood. Driving a car, as your father made plain, involved a good deal of responsibility. Goof up just once, and you'd lose the privilege for a month or so. You knew he meant it. You also knew that he was right. A car, handled recklessly, was dangerous in the extreme, and there were all too many daredevils.

What your own father didn't mention, your girlfriend's father would. She had to be home by 12 o'clock on weekends. You had to come to the house and pick her up, which meant coming in to talk for a while and putting up with smart remarks from her wretched little brother. Her Dad had pretty strict rules: absolutely no drinking at any time, call if you're going to be late, and, most importantly, drive safely!

Above: A side view of a 1957 Chevrolet Bel Air two-door hardtop. It had a quality of serene forward motion that appealed to a wide range of tastes, and was the perfect car to borrow from one's parents to impress an especially important 'date.'

At left: Two hot rods pull up to the starting line in a street-racing scene from the 1973 Universal motion picture *American Graffiti.* Note that the car at photo right is a 1932 Ford with updated running gear (and probably an intensely powerful engine)—a classic 'hot rod' in the purest sense, and a popular type of vehicle among drag racing purists of the 1950s.

CHOPPED, CHANNELED AND CUSTOMIZED

The sunny, never-never-land of California sprouts its own kind of unique lifestyle. Fenced off from the rest of the world by mountains on the east and the broad Pacific on the west, California is an island unto itself. In the 1950s, it was the place to be. California has always been synonymous with the good life, golden beaches, suntanned girls and surfing. There was a spirit of youth and freedom all across the country, which had its roots in these sun-drenched beaches. The kids were expressing themselves in ways that kids had never done before. There was that strange blend of music, called rock 'n' roll. There were black leather jackets and ducktail haircuts, flat tops and sunglasses, ponytails and sock hops. And there were cars—the fins, the chrome, the garish automobiles of the 1950s. Kids, ever striving for expression, took on the automobile as a kind of artistic expression, a way to be known in the world.

It was 'in' to be a nonconformist. The strong, silent types like James Dean were the heroes of the day. Wild cars were part of the image. The roaring exhausts and screeching brakes marked a true rebel of the road. There were those who toyed with engines, boring out cylinders and lengthening the stroke. There were others who worked on the exteriors, cutting and welding, painting and striping. One of the latter was George Barris.

Barris had been a child of the Depression. He'd been fascinated by cars then. When he acquired his first car, a 1925 Buick, much the worse for wear, George set to work. With care and love, he smoothed the dented fenders, sewed up the torn interior, and then, in a burst of exuberance, painted the car orange and blue with diagonal rainbow stripes. Naturally, no one can drive a car like that and not get noticed. George had found the path to instant fame!

His next creation had once been a 1929 Model A Ford. Barris added extra lights to the front of it, strange, winged ornaments and fox tails! To enhance his art, Barris hung around a local body shop. Here, he learned the arts of bending and shaping metal, grinding and cutting, torch welding and body paneling.

Customizing went into hibernation during World War II, but shortly after the war was over, Barris opened shop again. There weren't too many late-model cars around at the time, so Barris set to work on a 1936 Ford convertible.

First he removed the running boards. He molded new

American customizers take existing designs and alter them to suit highly individualized tastes. In the 1950s, the world of customizers and customized cars sometimes segued into that of hot rodders and hot rods.

Opposite: A lowered 1938 Chevrolet coupe, with a custom 'flame' paint job and custom wheels. Older cars were prime targets for 1950s customizers.

That customizing did not exclude foreign cars *owned* by Americans is attested by the elegant lines of the customized Jaguar *at right*.

taillights, emblems and door handles. And he chopped the top. When a customizer talked about chopping the top, he meant lowering the car's roof line by removing segments of the roof pillars. This resulted in a lower profile, a kind of rakish look sometimes, but sometimes it was just plain kooky. There were customers who carried the art of chopping so far that the windshield became only a slit!

Well, it was fun and 'Barris Kustoms' was by now a pretty well known landmark in the Los Angeles suburb where he lived, but fame came to the door as a result of a hot rod and custom car show held at the Los Angeles Armory. George's cars appeared in the first issue of a new magazine called *Hot Rod*. Nobody, least of all George Barris, had ever guessed how many people secretly longed to drive a blistering blue automobile with violet flames streaming out from the hood, chrome from ear to ear, and no door handles. Hollywood stars, always looking for

something a little different, came to Barris with their fantasies. With a wave of the magic welding torch, there it was: the hot rod a star always wanted. Barris built cars for many of the stars: Jayne Mansfield, Tony Curtis, Bobby Darin and Liberace, among others.

What was curious was that car manufacturers attended the shows. They made notes. They drew pictures. Some of these customizers had good ideas. In 1954, Barris brought out the *Gold Sahara*. It became famous across the nation and drew crowds wherever it was exhibited. The *Sahara* featured such things as bumper bullets, a checkered grille, thin-line rear fins and a spare tire well molded into the rear deck lid. The bumper bullets became famous on the Cadillac. Ford borrowed the checkered grille and the spare tire well appeared on the Chrysler Imperial three years later.

Though George Barris was probably the earliest and

The two touchstones of the customizer's art were both exemplified in 1950s cars: these were flamboyance—as in the paint job on the car that is imaged on page 63—and subtlety—as in the harmonious blending of line and paint scheme in the customized 1956 Ford Fairlane Victoria sedan *on these pages*.

Note how certain details have been smoothed over—there is no hood ornament, for instance, and door handles are cleverly hidden. The 1956 Ford's pleasant lines have been maximized by adding custom taillight chrome and custom fender skirts.

The normally chrome front and rear bumpers have been veiled in metallic blue—a touch that utilizes them to add to the impression of increased overall length. This car has also been 'channeled,' a process whereby the underside of the carbody is modified to lower it, making for less ground clearance and an emphasis on sleekness.

An opulent, finely-executed paint scheme further adds to this meticulously customized Ford's ambience of smooth, uninterrupted flow.

Above and above right: A highly customized 1954 Mercury convertible. Melded into the design are a 1952 DeSoto grille; a leaded-in, or 'nosed' (smoothed over) hood; lowered chassis; a chopped (lowered by cutting, always referring to areas above the beltline) windshield; custom hubcaps; custom interior, and *dozens*, if not *hundreds*, of coats of black lacquer.

At right: A strikingly customized 1958 Chevrolet Impala Sport Coupe. A new grille, Frenched-in (reconfigured and integralized) door handles, custom interior and custom wheels are part of the treatment given this car.

Opposite: Note the difference in the 'flame' paint job given this 1939 Ford and the scallop motif on the Chevrolet just discussed. Also, the 'Mooneyes' on the Ford's headlights symbolize of one of the late-1950s customizers' best suppliers, Moon Equipment Company.

best known of the professionals (he was often called King of the Customizers), there were others who became equally famous in their own territories. One of these was Darryl Starbird, who got started in his father's home workshop in Wichita, Kansas. Starbird's creations were known for their futuristic styling. Several of his cars sported a bubble top made of contoured plastic, an out-of-this-world design indeed. One of Starbird's designs even featured a double bubble. It had flip-down doors, three wheels and a single, large headlight. It was the closest thing one could find to a flying saucer in the 1950s.

Darryl Starbird won national recognition for his work. In 1959, he received the Top Body Achievement Award at the National Hot Rod Association's National Custom Car Show in Detroit. His entry was a 1956 Ford Thunderbird restyled in his own unique futuristic manner. His show cars all had surrealistic names like the *Predicta*, the *Forcasta*, the *Fantabula*—in character with their outer space styling.

Customizers at this time would take pieces of various automobiles and refashion the various fins, taillights, grilles and fenders into cars that were unlike anything else on the road. Was it simple welding shop finesse or real artistry? Perhaps a little of both went into these incredible pieces of machinery.

In the mid-1950s, deep in the heart of beautiful downtown Detroit, two very creative brothers named Larry and Mike Alexander operated an establishment they called Custom City. Here they plied their trade, taking standard production line cars and creating fantastic chariots of a kind never seen before. One of the cars that drew their attention was the 1956 Ford.

The 1956 Ford was all right, but really pretty tame looking when you got right down to it. The Alexanders made a new grille of Studebaker components, and installed a wraparound front bumper centered in the grille opening. They replaced the headlights with those of an Oldsmobile. It wasn't anything much, compared with the things Darryl Starbird did, but it was nice—the lines were clean and the workmanship was impeccable. The car was chosen by a national magazine as one of the 10 best custom cars built in 1956. The Alexanders had achieved a small measure of greatness, and a lot of business for Custom City.

Another West Coast artist was Gene Winfield, who hailed from Modesto, California. 'Windy' served a tour of duty during the Korean Conflict, but in spite of this, he and

Near opposite: A very tastefully customized 1959 Corvette.

Customizing reversed the usual procedure of modifying an ideal design to suit the market. Such ideal designs were known as 'dream cars' (see also pages 25 and 40).

Below: Buick's 1951 XP-300 dream car, with all-aluminum body and 315 hp, 216-ci (3.5 L) V-8.

Far opposite: The 1951 Buick LeSabre (see also page 25). Such dream car features as wraparound windshields eventually saw production.

a like-minded friend continued their customizing work while stationed in Japan. By 1955, Windy was back in the States and going strong once more. His sleek, clean-swept cars took awards left and right at custom shows. One of Winfield's most radical cars was a revamped 1949 Mercury. It had inlaid bumpers, sculptured wheel wells, quad vertical headlights that were molded into the fenders, a tubular 'floating' grille, and a front seat that swung out when the car door was opened. The name of this imaginative creation was the *Solar Scene*.

When Darryl Starbird opened his shop in Wichita, he worked with another young customizer named Bill Cushenbery. Cushenbery was soon infected with California fever and went West to Monterey. There, his customized 1940 Ford coupe would become one of the more memora-

ble creations of the era. Cushenbery chopped the top and sectioned the body to form a very low profile. Called *El Matador*, the car featured canted, quad headlights and a rolled pan and a contoured rear body section. It was, however the very low silhouette that made the car so exciting.

There were a whole series of 'art forms' that grew up around the business of customizing. Each customizer had his own specialty. Paint was one thing that first caught the eye. There were the wild metallic colors that seemed to have unlimited depth. There were fanciful trims like pin-striping. Pin-striping—delicate, swirling, undulating lines that fanned across hood, around windows, headlights, trunks—was the mark of an artist. Pin-striping evolved into flame painting. Flames started out as little flickers shooting out from the hood. Like wildfire, the idea caught on and the

flames spread to engulf the entire car. A real artist, using a range of colors from yellow through brilliant orange-red, could make the flames look almost real. This kind of work took hours of time. Patient blending of colors and hand rubbing were required to get exactly the right touch. The flames then evolved into scalloping.

Scalloping was more subdued than the flames. It was more stylized, more elegant. Done with care by a consummate artist, scalloping would have looked appropriate even on the local banker's car.

The metal workers were artists in another medium. They worked with cutting tools and welding torches. The cars they produced reveal a lot about the 1950s. There was a sense of fun, of fantasy and sometimes a little tongue-in-cheek humor. Just imagine a 1950 Ford coupe with the following embellishments: quad headlights; taillights from

Opposite: A customized 1932 Ford roadster, with freshly upgraded chromework, gleaming red paint, altered suspension and custom wheels. No doubt, a carefully-crafted custom interior fills the passenger compartment.

Under its hood might be found anything from an upgraded version of its original 'flathead' V-8, or a competition-equipped, overhead-valve power plant with vastly higher output.

At left: A 1938 Chevrolet sedan with glossy red paint, refurbished footpads on the running boards, custom removable front fender guard, refurbished chromework, custom interior and other fine detailing that place it in the category of carefully crafted custom cars.

There was often creative interchange between customizers and automakers.

Such features as were found on the 1956 Oldsmobile dream car, the Golden Rocket (above)—including specially-crafted fiberglass body and metallic gold paint—may have originated in a customizer's fertile imagination.

Of course, the opposite could also be true, as a customizer might covet the Golden Rocket's entry system, in which the seats automatically swiveled outward for easier access when the doors were opened.

a 1957 Olds 98; floating grille; exhaust pipes that extend along the side rocker panels; no door handles; and a body with completely smooth, sculpted, clean lines. The color of the car is deep red. Inside, everything is padded in wine and white vinyl. The trunk is padded in white vinyl and carpeted with wine red carpeting. Nestled in the recesses of the trunk is a TV, so you need not miss American Bandstand while on your picnic. The TV operates on a voltage converter, as this was before the age of the portable TV.

Customizing was a kind of 'bits and pieces' operation in one sense. First there was the basic car—a 1950 Chevrolet, for instance—very ordinary. How would it look with a different grille? A customizer might take the grille teeth from a

1953 Chevy and install them in a molded-in grille shell. This was better, but only a beginning.

The headlights were the next thing to go. Installed in their place were a pair of lights from a 1955 Oldsmobile. Next the hood was 'nosed' and slightly reshaped. (Nosing was a term which meant all chrome, including hood ornaments had been removed and all the holes had been filled in.) Then the car would be channeled. (Channeled referred to the lowering of a car's body so that it appeared to be floating just slightly above the ground.)

Chromed exhaust pipes running from the front wheels along the sides of the car to the rear wheels were another touch many customizers added. For taillights, how about

those of a 1954 Mercury, inverted and mounted low in the rear fenders? For further interest, the rear would be decked. (Decking meant that all the rear trim and chrome would be removed and again, all the holes would be filled.)

Much of the customizer's art lay in attention to details. Unusual hub caps, bumpers, skirts on the rear wheel wells and pleated upholstery added to a one-of-a-kind look. The final touch was, of course, the paint job. Metallic paints and lacquers took hours of painstaking labor. Purple was a color much in vogue, because it was so striking. Candy-apple red was another. Add flames or scalloping, pin-striping–even cartooning– and you had a truly unique automobile.

Customizing was a labor of love. It took hours to complete each modification, particularly if you chose to do the

Below: A Buick dream car for the year 1956, called the Centurion. It could carry four passengers, and those in the rear seats had only to push on the respective front bucket seat, and it would move forward to allow easier exiting.

General Motors put on yearly auto shows called Motoramas, where they displayed their dream cars and received much valuable commentary to help guide their styling approach to the auto market.

Near opposite: The 1956 Motorama, with Buick Centurion and Chevrolet Impala (near) dream cars in evidence.

Such cars as the customized late-1938 Chevrolet Master Deluxe sedan shown *above* would appear in car shows put on by customizers and major auto parts manufacturers.

Opposite: A customized Ford Model A four-door sedan. Some customizers preferred to leave their cars looking almost stock, with paint jobs that closely mimicked original hues.

Custom wheels and lowered bodies have always been a giveaway, as have been the usual, highly suspect, twin exhaust pipes emitting a throaty rumble.

work yourself. In the 1950s, a great many people did their own customizing because of the expense of a professional job and because it was fun. Customizing your own automobile might take three or four years and several thousand dollars, but the results were worth every minute of time. Driving around in such a car made you king of the hill with all your friends and was an aesthetic treat.

In a way, customizing was a kind of recycling process, using as it did so many parts and accessories from various cars. The auto graveyards of America were a customizer's gold mine. With cutting torch, wrench, screwdriver and a little pocket money, you could obtain enough 'goodies' to

produce any fantasy you had in mind. The exhilaration of a visit to the local junk yard was matched only by being invited to participate in the Saturday night drag races.

Though some forms of customizing were really on the wild side with extravagant shapes, colors and interiors, much of it– at least in the early to mid-1950s–was rather conservative. Much of it was also a vast improvement over the original styling. (This is probably the reason so many auto designers attended the custom shows and made notes!) In view of the art forms of the 1960s–such as Andy Warhol's Campbell's Soup cans–what the customizers did with the automobile was really a forerunner of pop art.

DAYTONA, BONNEVILLE AND POINTS SOUTH

Americans, from time immemorial, have loved racing. Horse racing must have been one of the earliest sports in the Colonies, since wagering on the races was so often a punishable offense. Every nineteenth century county fair had its horse races, and there were more than a few impromptu 'races' by stalwart and respectable deacons and pious church members on Sunday mornings in those early days.

The very first gasoline-powered automobile ever to chug down the road in the United States was built by the Duryea brothers from Illinois. It was the summer of 1893 when this marvel made its debut. With its four hp, one-cylinder engine and its weight of 750 pounds, the car moved at an easy walking pace. With time, however, and with modifications and improvements, it was able to travel all of 10 mph. Three years after its first slow-moving appearance, the Duryea went into production. In that year, 1896, 10 of these 'horseless carriages' were sold to intrepid buyers. It was an era of inventors, however, and a great many people were probing the possibilities of the motor car.

The first automobile race occurred in France on 22 July 1894. News of the race inspired American auto builders to emulate it. The first American car race ever held was sponsored by HH Kohlsaat, the publisher of the Chicago *Times Herald*. It began at nine o'clock in the morning on a cold, snowy Thanksgiving Day in 1895. Six cars appeared at the starting line, which was blanketed in heavy snow. During the race three cars broke down, one collided with a horse-drawn hack and one driver passed out from the cold. A Duryea, despite losing its way and breaking down, managed to finish the race, and even won. Its official time was 54 miles in 10 hours, 23 minutes. One other car, a German Benz, completed that momentous race, an hour and a half behind the Duryea.

All along, racing has been important in the development of the automobile, not because of the prizes, but because of the recognition that winners receive. As Henry Ford once said, 'Winning or making a record is the best kind of advertising.' By the early 1900s, many kinds of auto races flourished. People held races on city streets, converted horse tracks and on country roads. Hill-climbing events, like those held at Pikes Peak, Eagle Rock and Mt Washington, spurred adventurous drivers to try their luck. Record-breaking events also became popular. The first race at the

Not only were racing competitions held in the 1950s, but endurance and economy trials were also popular. These were sources of good publicity for automakers' products.
At right: A Ford, a Plymouth and a Chevrolet (all 1957 models) finish the last segment of the 'Big Run' endurance trial on 10 May 1957, in San Francisco.
The Mobilgas Economy Run was the most well known of the economy trials. *Opposite:* A celebration surrounds a Studebaker that won Class One in the 1952 Mobilgas Economy Run.

Not much different than hot rodders, the people who ran moonshine drove modified versions of everyday cars. This led to the development of 'stock car racing' as a sport.

Below: A suspicious-looking Buick with non-stock hubcaps.

Opposite: A lowered 1955 Mercury Montclair hardtop with 'moon' hubcaps. There was an abundance of performance parts to boost the power of its 292-ci (4.7 L) V-8, and ample room in the trunk for 'moonshine' tanks.

Indianapolis Speedway was held in 1909. Auto manufacturers used this event to promote sales of their cars, but they were not alone. All the industry suppliers–tire companies, makers of shock absorbers, carburetors and headlights–used the racing triumphs as promotional opportunities.

Racing continued in the United States through the 1920s and even the dismal times of the 1930s. During World War II, racing all but ceased. In the late 1940s, however, a gas station attendant named Bill France decided to devote his talents to developing the sport of stock car racing. In addition to being a mechanic, Bill had often done some stock car racing on the side.

Stock car racing, in those days, was mainly confined to the Southeastern states. There was an interesting reason for this. Stock car racing had its roots in the honored Southern tradition of 'moonshining.' It was a well-known fact that local bootleggers had long held the advantage over the government 'revenuers,' knowing as they did every uncharted back road and byway in the county. Tax collection has always been one of the more imaginative branches of government, and 'revenuers,' by their nature, were among the more sporting types of bureaucrats.

To improve their odds at catching the rum-runners, the government men developed some very crafty auto-

mobiles. The word got around. The opposition, naturally, did some very fancy tinkering of its own. Local mechanics probed the possibilities of the factory-built engine. It is hard to believe that sport didn't play a part in this earlier. Delivering moonshine served as a training ground for some of the early stock car drivers. All the techniques of racing and evasion–high-speed turns, power slides and braking–were used in running moonshine. When they weren't evading revenuers, 'the boys' would set up an impromptu race on an oval horse track.

Bill France, who had done some of the engine work as well as driving in stock car races, set about to regulate specifications for stock cars and improve benefits for drivers. In 1946, France asked the AAA Contest Board to sanction a 100-mile championship stock car race at Charlotte, North Carolina. The board declined to sanction the race, so in December of 1947 Bill France and a group of stock car fans formed the National Association for Stock Car Racing, known ever since as NASCAR.

NASCAR caught the imagination of racing fans in the 1950s. There was a kind of democracy in stock car racing that suited the times. Grassroots Americans have always been a little suspicious of things European. Here was an American kind of race with American cars driven by good old boys from back home, who would never use one of those temperamental Italian cars–and foreign cars were not allowed to compete, after all. The excitement of these races came from the showings of such cars as the Buick Century, the Olds Eighty-Eight and Chrysler 300–all the pride of Detroit. Drivers like Fireball Roberts, and the father and son team of Lee and Richard Petty, became revered folk heroes.

In the South, particularly, stock car racing pre-empted both baseball and football as the most popular sport. Its popularity spread in the 1950s from the hills of East Tennessee and the North Carolina back country, all the way to Kansas, Oklahoma and points West. Every small, rural town boasted of Friday night stock car races. It kept the kids off the street, and it also enthralled their elders. Many racers of the 1950s found the stock car races a perfect way to exercise the urge to tinker with an engine and to race legally. Winners could count on being the hometown hero–at least until the next race. Some of the racers graduated to bigger and better things. Gordon Johncock, who started out in stock car races in Michigan and Indiana,

Below: Exemplifying the blend of power and heaviness in cars of its day is this 1951 Cadillac Series 62 sedan, weighing 4102 pounds, with a 331-ci (5.4 L) V-8 of 160 hp.

While Chrysler was making a name on the stock car tracks with its potent 'hemi' V-8s, the company was also making its mark in the appropriate class categories of the Mobilgas Economy Run (see also pages 76–77).

Opposite: A young California Chrysler dealer with a Mobilgas Economy Run trophy and the car he won it with—a 1958 Chrysler New Yorker, powered by a 345-hp, 392-ci (6.4 L) 'hemi' V-8.

went on to Indianapolis. Besides, these races were exciting, perhaps even more so than the 'big' races, because so many ordinary people were personally involved.

What should be emphasized about all cars of the 1950s is that they were big, heavy automobiles in comparison with today's cars. They featured heavy frames and bodies of heavy-gauge steel. To think of such hulks on the race track seems ludicrous. The engines for these monsters, however, were built for power and performance, and perform they did—with breathtaking ability. Chrysler's hemi-head V-8 was a legendary power plant. Some racers who modified the hemi were able to get as much as 1000 hp (for very short periods) from its lionhearted engine. The Chrysler 300, born in 1955, dominated NASCAR racing in the mid-1950s.

A Cadillac would certainly never be considered a racing car—or would it? The 1950 series 61 was a relatively light car, which came equipped with standard transmission and a 160 V-8 engine. According to some drivers, it was the fastest passenger car in the United States at that time. Proof might be seen in the results of the Le Mans race for 1950. A near-stock Coupe de Ville and a Cadillac equipped with a special body came in tenth and eleventh overall, ludicrous as Cadillac at Le Mans may seem. An Allard J-2, powered by the same Cadillac V-8 engine, came in third. Racing did not really fit the Cadillac image, though, so Cadillac engines were often raced in the bodies of other cars. 'Fordillac' and 'Studillac' were two hybrids designed by Bill Frick. Briggs Cunningham and Phil Walters once 'stuffed' a Cadillac engine into an Austin-

Healy. The resulting automobile took a first and second at Watkins Glen! Thereupon, Cadillac refused to sell Cunningham any more engines.

There were other cars whose manufacturers weren't so stuffy about 'prestige': the Buick Century and the Olds Eighty-Eight. The Hudson Hornet, a rather *zaftig*, if aerodynamically sound, automobile was outstanding in AAA and NASCAR racing until the mid-1950s. The Hudson Hornet was an interesting car from the standpoint of stock car racing. The Hornet came equipped with a brawny 308-ci (five L) six-cylinder engine. With its 3.8 x 4.5 bore and stroke, it was capable of something like 145 bhp at 3800 rpm in stock form, but in the hands of a precision tuner, it was capable of much more.

Such a tuner was Marshall Teague. Teague claimed he could get 121 mph from a certified 'stock' Hornet. Aided by Hudson engineers, Teague proved his ideas in the 1952 AAA season, which he finished with a 1000 point lead over his nearest rival. Engineers at Hudson, fired with enthusiasm for Teague's ideas, had introduced a series of 'severe usage' options that were actually nothing more than disguised racing modifications. Twin-H power, which was offered for the first time in 1952, consisted of twin carburetors and a dual manifold induction, never before offered on a six-cylinder. The 7-X racing engine arrived late in 1953. Modifications included over-bored cylinders (.020), a special cam and head, larger valves and higher compression. The 7-X was just what Marshall Teague needed. A true racing engine, it had 210 bhp. In 1953, NASCAR drivers like Herb Thomas, Frank Mundy, Al Keller and Dick Rathmann won 21 races driving the modified Hornet.

In those years, very few cars outran the Hudson Hornet. One that came close was the Chrysler New Yorker. The stock New Yorker, with its powerful hemi engine, could make zero to 60 in 10 seconds. Flat out, it could achieve at least 110 mph, a ferocious competitor for the Hornet...but not quite good enough. Then came the big 300 in 1955, which delivered 300 bhp as a modified stock engine. The Chrysler 300 was a legend in NASCAR racing in those years. It probably would have remained a dominant force in NASCAR if the Automobile Manufacturers Association had not decided to de-emphasize racing.

Another of the powerful sedans that took to racing was the Oldsmobile. Engineers introduced the first Rocket Eighty-Eight engine in 1949. The Rocket Eighty-Eight was

Below: **Advertisement for the 1952 Hudson Hornet—with a 308-ci (five L) six-cylinder of 145 hp and 425 foot-pounds of torque. The 7-X racing version had 340 ci (5.5 L).**
Opposite: **A 1950 Oldsmobile Eighty-Eight Holiday coupe, equipped with the 303-ci (4.9 L) Rocket V-8, with 135 hp in factory trim.**

one of those landmark designs so typical of the 1950s. It was so far ahead of its time that even today, over 40 years later, most large American cars are powered by engines like the Rocket Eighty-Eight. Specifications for the engine include 303.7-ci (4.9 L) displacement, a compression ratio of between 7.5:1 and 8:1 and stroke of 3.75 x 3.44 inches and a torque of 240 foot-pounds initially. Oldsmobile had originally planned to use the Rocket only in the Olds Ninety-Eight model, but opted for using the engine in the

Eighty-Eight as well. The Rocket in the lighter Eighty-Eight was a natural for NASCAR racing. As a stock car, the Olds Eighty-Eight proved itself in no uncertain terms. In its first year of competition, the Eighty-Eight was entered in nine NASCAR grand nationals. Of those nine, the Olds Eighty-Eights won six. At the Daytona Time Trials in 1950, an Eighty-Eight broke the speed record for its class with a two-way average speed of 100.28 mph.

There were other races in the 1950s. One that has been nearly hidden by the mists of time was called officially the Carrera Panamericana. To aficionados and racing drivers, it was known more simply as the Mexican Road Race. It was international in scope and covered a distance of 2178 miles in 1950, the year it was first run. An Oldsmobile Eighty-Eight driven by Hershel McGriff won the race. McGriff's average speed was 77.43 mph. Running against such formidable European contenders as Alfa-Romeo, the Olds had truly proved itself in this grueling race.

In subsequent years, this course was shortened to a distance of 1934 miles. The strong and durable Lincoln, with its innovative ball-joint front suspension, dominated those rugged miles. Running in the International Standard Class, Lincolns had no peer. Lincolns took the top five places in the Mexican Road Race in 1952. In 1953, this so-called luxury sedan picked up the top four places, and in 1954, a first and second place.

Today, the thought of such an automobile competing in a road race at all is laughable. The fact that Lincoln won and won consistently, is incredible. How was it possible? Part of it was due to the superior valve-in-head V-8 engine. An even larger part was due to the race preparation Lincolns received.

Clay Smith was a mechanic with a magic touch. It was his job to 'prep' the Lincolns for the arduous Mexican Road Race. The Ford Motor Company, eager for the publicity that winning the race would bring, had none of the compunctions about racing that Cadillac suffered. After obtaining Smith's services as a mechanic, the company went all out to see that he had the best materials with which to work. Thus, Lincolns were equipped with 'export' suspension, Ford truck camshafts, mechanical valve lifters, special hubs and front wheel spindles. To this list was also added the choice of two optional rear ends.

What is truly incredible, is that Lincoln, equipped with a higher axle and a stock engine, could top 130 mph! Chuck

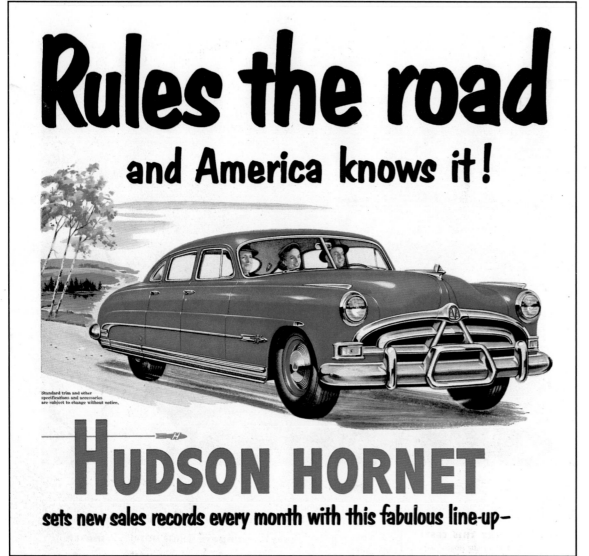

Rules the road
and America knows it!

Standard trim and other specifications and accessories are subject to change without notice.

HUDSON HORNET
sets new sales records every month with this fabulous line-up—

Above: Promotional art for 1955 Oldsmobiles of the Eighty-Eight series. Such advertisements as this further expanded the image that was being created by each manufacturer for its cars on the race tracks of America.

Opposite: A 1955 Oldsmobile Eighty-Eight. The standard Eighty-Eight was powered by a 324-ci overhead-valve V-8 of 185 hp, while cars designated 'Super Eighty-Eight' had an upgraded version of the same base engine, producing 202 hp. Competition versions of same would produce upwards of 250 hp.

Stevenson, who won the race in 1952, finished nearly an hour ahead of the Ferrari, which had won the race the year before. Clay Smith was killed in a tragic accident in 1954, the last year of the Mexican Road Race.

A little-known fact about the Mexican Road Race is that in addition to Oldsmobile and Lincoln, Dodge also turned in an outstanding performance in the race. In 1954, Dodge took over the Medium Stock class. Dodge, noted for its high-efficiency engine, took the first, second, third, fourth, sixth and ninth positions, an excellent record for such a difficult marathon.

Not much is written or remembered of the Mexican Road Race now, but in the early 1950s, when racing was gaining a foothold in the public's imagination, the Carrera Panamericana represented all the glamour and hard-driving a race could be.

Daytona Beach, Florida, has been associated with automobiles and racing since 1902, when Alexander Winton and RE Olds first raced on the sands of Ormond Daytona. The brief 15-mile stretch of sand established Daytona as the place to try for land speed records. Daytona held sway for nearly 30 years, until racers discovered the salt flats of Utah. With alarm, city fathers in Daytona envisioned a western exodus. In 1936, Sig Haugdahl, a former Daytona record-holder, was called in to offer suggestions. Daytona, after all, was a tourist attraction, and tourists meant cash money. The city fathers didn't want to see a good thing die.

Haugdahl's solution was amazingly simple. Take one and one-half miles of sandy beach plus one and one-half miles of parallel blacktop highway and join each section by a one-tenth mile connecting road, and what do you get? Roughly an oval track running about 3.2 miles. With a little advertising and a $5000 purse, the Daytona Track lured an Indianapolis winner, Bill Cummings; a couple of dirt track stars, Doc Mackenzie and Bob Sall; a British race driver, Major Goldie Gardiner; midget auto racing champion Bill Schindler; and future NASCAR pioneer Bill France.

The AAA Board had sanctioned a 250-mile race, but the city fathers had forgotten one thing: with all the 'heavy traffic,' the two dirt connecting roads soon became impossible and impassable. The race was called at 200 miles when tow trucks could no longer dislodge all the bogged-down vehicles fast enough to keep the course open. Such was the running of the first Daytona stock car race.

With the end of World War II, Daytona Speed Week,

which occurred in February, came into full bloom. There was a new track, a few miles south of the 1936 landmark. It included, as did the old track, a combination beach and highway course running a distance of 4.1 miles. Time trials were again held on the beach as in the early days of automobile racing. Running the Daytona Time Trials became an important part of winter vacation for many race car enthusiasts. After all the formal competition runs, NASCAR allowed the tourists a moment of glory. For the sum of 12 dollars, you could take your own Chrysler hemi or hot Buick on an officially timed run across the sand. Those who recorded better than 100 mph became members of the Century Club. Nothing could have done more to fire the public's enthusiasm for Daytona.

Speed Week in the mid-1950s was dominated by NASCAR competition. The 1955 Grand National was won by Tim Flock driving a Chrysler 300. Flock's closest competitor was Lee Petty, also driving a Chrysler. Third place went to a Buick Century, followed by two Olds Eighty-Eights for fourth and fifth. Fireball Roberts, driving another Buick, had appeared to dominate the race. NASCAR officials, however, declared Robert's car illegal since the engine's push rods had been altered. The most famous race on the track was known as the Daytona 500. As one of the best-known tracks of that era, it regularly drew crowds of 100,000 or more.

Stock car racing had really come of age at this point and much of its prestige was due to the efforts of Bill France. As previously mentioned, France had been both a mechanic and a race car driver since the early 1930s. Stock car racing in the years before the Second World War had grown rapidly and had gotten out of hand. Under the chaotic conditions which existed then, drivers were at the mercy of unscrupulous promoters who would often 'skip town' with the gate receipts, leaving behind unpaid bills and drivers' purses. Some mechanics also belonged to a slippery bunch who knew how to cheat the drivers for profit. Safety standards and rules were rarely well enforced. France set out to clean up and promote stock car racing in the late 1940s. To combat these conditions and to give the sport of stock car racing respectability, Bill France founded NASCAR.

The first speedway built especially for NASCAR races was opened in Darlington, South Carolina, in 1950. The track, one and one-eighth miles long with high banked

turns, was eyed pessimistically by many. Who would want to travel to a little hick town on the outskirts of nowhere just to see a 500-mile race? Could any of the entrants last 500 miles? Nevertheless, NASCAR's first 500 miler was run in Darlington and was, despite all misgivings, quite successful. Darlington, along with Daytona, Charlotte, Rockingham, Atlanta and Talladega, became known for its outstanding NASCAR speedway.

Speed records have always been a part of racing. In the early days before and after World War I, it was the sandy Daytona Beach strip that provided an area for land speed records. It is hard to believe that 85 years ago when automobiles were still in their infancy, Frank Marriott, driving a Stanley Steamer with what looked like oversized bicycle tires, broke the land speed record at 129 mph. This is nothing at all when compared to the records set by the daring Malcolm Campbell in his famous Bluebird. Sir Malcolm's exploits will be legendary for as long as speed records are attempted.

In 1935, the speed record was 276.82 mph. Sir Malcolm made his first run over the famous salt flats at Bonneville,

Opposite: **A 1951 Lincoln Cosmopolitan club coupe. While Lincoln stood at the top of Ford Motor Company's offerings, the rather stately car was not immune to modification for racing, as it sported Ford's largest power plant of the time — a 336-ci (5.5 L) 'flathead' V-8 with 154 hp output in factory form.**

As a matter of fact, the popular phrase 'hot rod Lincoln' came into parlance after the performance crowd had had its way with such marvels of early-1950s machinery.

Below: **A 1954 Dodge Royal hardtop. Equipped with the 241-ci (3.9 L) version of the Chrysler 'hemi' V-8, it was not quite the terror of the track even in competition form.**

However, the 1955 Chrysler 300, with a 300-hp, 331-ci (5.4 L) 'hemi' V-8 in street form, did, when tuned for racing, put Chrysler in the lead.

Below: A 1956 Buick Century four-door hardtop, a car that was both likely and unlikely to appear in a drag race—likely, because it was very flashy, and unlikely, because it had a 322-ci (5.2 L) V-8 under its hood that was designed for smoothness, not brutal torque, and was further hampered by Buick transmission design, which also featured smoothness at the expense of efficiency.

By contrast, the 1955 Chevrolet Bel Air sedan shown *opposite* was designed for snappy response, with its efficient 265-ci (4.4 L) V-8 mated to a no-nonsense Chevrolet transmission. When modified by a knowing 'hot rodder,' as with this example, such a car could respond well, indeed.

Utah, late in 1935. On his first run, he established a speed in excess of 300 mph. Campbell continued to break many land speed records at Bonneville and by 1947 the land speed record at Bonneville was 400 mph. Sir Malcolm died in 1949, having held the land speed record nine different times throughout his career. The Bluebird and her daring driver served as inspiration for a new generation of record breakers, including Mickey Thompson, the legend of the late 1950s.

But what about California? Was the mecca of 'auto-mania' out of the racing picture? Decidedly not–but with a different twist. Stock car racing never achieved the popularity there that it did in the South and Midwest, but the West Coast invented its own unique form of organized racing–drag racing.

Drag racing is unlike either stock car racing or sports car racing. The cars run two at a time, side by side. It's a standing start contest between evenly matched cars, the sole objective being to see which car crosses a finish line

1320 feet away first. It takes a certain type of person to enjoy these races. The race is over in a few seconds and the overall winner is determined by a series of 'eliminations.' Nearly eight million fans pay to attend these races every year, and they are becoming even more popular.

Drag racing in the 1950s was only a half-serious sport. Car buffs of the 1950s couldn't resist the lure of speed. They puttered around in their free time, combining automobile chassis and frames with V-8 engines in the hope of coming up with the ultimate fast car. Racing such cars on public thoroughfares, as they sometimes did, was dangerous.

Rather than totally discourage drag racing, Wally Parks and several others civilized it instead. Founding the National Hot Rod Association (NHRA), Parks organized drag meets on unused airport runways. The runways were about one-half to three-quarters of a mile long. A quarter of a mile was the limit a driver could accelerate and stop, so it became the official distance.

THE CREAM OF THE CROP

Never before in automotive history had designers and engineers been so innovative. There was great freedom to experiment and to develop new ideas. Competition was keen among the manufacturers. The model changeover was a time of high excitement for everyone. It was called by its detractors, 'planned obsolescence': the idea, real or imagined, that last year's automobile could not hold a candle to this year's new model. Thus, one manufacturer might come up with an excellent design, but three years was the maximum time that design would be produced–more likely it would only be on the market for two years before another major restyling.

There were cars in these years that were classic in their beauty. Cars so incredibly sculpted, so sleek and clean-lined that they invite admiration and imitation even today.

One of these classics was the Studebaker Loewy Coupe. Studebaker was the oldest automobile manufacturer in the nation. It had been in business since the time of horse-drawn carriages. This South Bend, Indiana, company celebrated its centennial in 1952. Car sales had been falling for the independent company. The manufacturer blamed it on Korean Conflict restrictions, but this was probably only the tip of the iceberg so far as internal problems were concerned. Clearly the company needed a car that would boost its sagging sales.

For the 1953 model year, Raymond Loewy's design studios introduced the Commander and Champion, Starliner hardtop and Starlight coupe. The designs were those of chief designer, Robert E Bourke, who had intended them to be special show models at first. Loewy, who had a different vision for the designs, sold them to the Studebaker management who adopted the styles for their 1953 models. The lines of these cars were faultless. Having none of the garish chrome or over-done trim, none of the boxy lines so typical of its competitors, the Studebaker Champions and Commanders were elegantly simple with a European look. Eventually, these cars were lauded as the pre-eminent automotive design of the decade.

Unfortunately, Studebaker experienced a delay in production due to model changeover. When they finally did get underway, it was discovered that management had read the market wrong. Demand for the magnificent coupe was four times greater than for the sedan model that man-

Studebaker had success with its postwar 'propeller-nose' models, an example of which is the 1951 Commander coupe advertised *at right*.

When Studebaker went public with its 1953 model cars—designed by the Loewy studios—it amazed the world. In fact, the design, which has become known as the 'Loewy Coupe,' was internationally recognized as *the* design of the decade.

Opposite: A 1953 Studebaker Starliner coupe, evidencing the elegantly simple 'Loewy Coupe' design.

See and drive this 120-horsepower wonder car!

Great new Studebaker Commander V-8

agement had thought would be its top seller. It took weeks to switch over to production of the coupe, and much valuable time and many sales were lost.

The series was offered again for the model year 1954, the only change being the egg-crate grille. However, production woes still besieged the company and, due to problems with management and cost of production, less than 70,000 cars were produced for the entire year. Robert Bourke, as a matter of curiosity, priced out one of his Commander Starliners according to the cost used by General Motors. The results were shocking. Had the Commander been a Chevrolet, it would have sold for $1900; as a Studebaker, it was selling for $2502. These were the years in which a price war was being fought between Ford and GM. Neither company really injured the other; it was small, independent companies, like Studebaker, which suffered irretrievable losses. Packard, at this time, bought out Studebaker and the company became known as Studebaker-Packard. The rest is history. The classic 'Loewy Coupes' stand yet as a reminder of the excellence that was possible in the 'era of fins and chrome.'

The Ford Motor Company had long produced a model called the Lincoln Continental, a luxurious car much beloved by many dealers and customers alike. However, Lincoln Continentals were taken off the market in 1948 and there seemed little likelihood that they would ever be reborn. Then in the mid-1950s, due to much pressure from dealers and customers, Ford brought out a separate division called simply Continental. In developing the Continental, Ford's goal was to establish dominance in the high- priced field of automobiles, and especially to dominate Cadillac.

In 1956, the first Mark II Continental cost $10,000– $10,000 of sheer perfection, flawless in every line and exquisitely built. It was the only model Continental produced for that year and the following year. The lines were crisp, slightly rakish, clean and elegant. It had been three years in development. The project, under the direction of William Clay Ford (Henry Ford II's younger brother) had called in a distinguished group of consultants to submit their ideas: Buzz Grisinger, Reese Miller, Vince Gardener, George Walker (who later became Ford's design chief) and Walter Buell Ford (no relation to the other Fords). Their designs were nice, but somehow they were just not right.

In the end, Ford management reviewed 13 different presentations before they finally selected a design from

The 1956 Continental Mark II was large, at 4825 pounds, but the simplicity and balance of its lines dealt with its size brilliantly.

Acclaimed abroad, it was not a big seller in the US. *Above:* A 1956 Continental Mark II. (Compare with the 'standard' 1956 Lincoln on page 43.)

The difference between the 1956 and 1957 model years was that the 1957, at 4797 pounds, had a lighter frame.

At right and opposite: Views of a 1957 Mark II. In addition to the Sport Coupe model, a convertible variant was offered—of which just two cars were manufactured and delivered.

Reinhart, Buehrig and Thomas of Special Products. The car was regal in its simplicity. Harley Copp, who was chief engineer for Special Products, drew up a special chassis frame of steel rails. They dipped low between the wheels, allowing the car to have chair-height seats, but at the same time keeping the roof line relatively low. The cockpit and dash were inspired by aircraft designs, and were sharply delineated and devoid of ornament. The engine was the Lincoln 368-ci V-8 (6.0 L) capable of 285 to 300 hp at 4600 rpm. The car measured 218.5 inches long and rode on a 126-inch wheelbase. It attracted wide-eyed admiration in both Europe and America, and was a car truly in a class by itself.

Despite its classic beauty, the Continental Mark II was not a blazing success in the marketplace. The word from the sales division was that Mark II had not made a difference in production. While a few wealthy customers had switched to the Mark II, many more with less cash were still buying Cadillacs instead of Lincolns. There were price cuts to boost sales. Subsequently, Mark IIIs, Mark IVs and Mark Vs were introduced, but none had the lines or the beauty of the original Mark II, although some sold a little better. The Continental division faded quietly with the close of the 1950s. The Mark II Continental, a car on a par with the great Duesenberg, will be remembered always as one of the outstanding automobiles of the decade.

The Packard was a car with a reputation. Throughout the 1920s and into the 1930s, Packards had been one of the leading luxury cars. People remembered with nostalgia the Packard Speedster model 734, a sleek roadster which

When the beautiful Continental Mark II design failed to work miracles in the marketplace, Ford's Lincoln Division created less timeless Continental designs more in tune with the 1950s.

The 1958 Continental Mark III (below) was the first of these. Compare this bulky design with the Continental Mark IIs shown on pages 92–93.

The end of this progression was the 1960 Continental Mark V (opposite), which was replaced in 1961 by a car that was as brilliant as the Mark II —but the 1961 Continental must be left to another book.

A car that became, in retrospect, emblematic of the late 1950s was the 'shark-finned' 1959 Cadillac, with its twin bullet taillights like the transfixed afterburner flames of some Earth-bound starship blazing away on either side of each fin.

Below: A 1959 Cadillac Series 6200 four-door sedan, with tailfins trailing into the background.

Opposite: A 1959 Cadillac Series 62 hardtop coupe. A 325-hp, 390-ci (6.3 L) V-8 was the motive power for such a car, and standard features included power brakes and power steering; and options included six-way power seats, power windows, air conditioning and Cruise Control.

retailed in 1929 for $5210. It was definitely not a car for the masses. However, luxury cars in the Great Depression were hit hard, and the Packard Company suffered huge losses. To carry the company along, management switched to building less expensive cars. This unfortunate policy continued after World War II.

The Packard of 1950 was described as a 'pregnant elephant.' The design was a heavy and ungainly postwar 'aerodynamic' style, not attractive and not popular. For 1951, the company went for total restyling, employing John Reinhart (who would later be remembered for the Mark II Continental). The lines were elegant, far and away from the bulbous 1950 model. Though the company still maintained its low-priced line, some of the models being built at this time were reflective of the wonderful old luxury cars. These were the 250s, the 300s and the 400s.

Basically, they were what their forerunners had been: well-built, ultimately comfortable, high-powered road cars. The 300s and 400s were mounted on a 127-inch wheelbase; the 250s used the shorter 122-inch wheelbase for its Mayfair hardtop and convertible. The 250s were

sporty cars which had a lot of appeal for the public. Despite all this, some of the Packard aura had been lost. The Packard, once associated with wealthy millionaires, had somehow lost class.

James Nance became president of Packard in 1952. It was hoped by one and all that Nance could invigorate the flagging company. Nance wanted to return to the days of luxury formal sedans and limousines.

He proposed that the low-priced 200 models be turned into a separate line called the Clipper, which first appeared as a separate make in 1956. In 1953, Packard brought out the Patrician which featured a leather-covered top and tiny rear windows, plus an equally elegant interior. The Patrician sold for $6531, a price that ranked it with luxury cars like Cadillacs and Lincolns. In that same year, the Caribbean, an elegant, beautifully styled convertible, was also introduced. Limited to 750 cars, the Caribbean outsold Cadillac's rival model, the Eldorado.

Packard might well have regained its old glory, had the company not purchased the Studebaker plant in South Bend. Packard, at this point, though small, was healthy. Studebaker, on the other hand, was plagued with problems, the largest being high overhead and low productivity.

Nevertheless, in 1955, Packard brought out a car that was a technological marvel. A top feature was Torsion-Level suspension, which consisted of an interlinked torsion bar system that operated on all four wheels. The suspension could correct for any load, thanks to a complex electrical system and the interlinking torsion bar. The ride such a system delivered was like velvet, and the handling was in true Packard character. Moreover, there was a new and powerful V-8 engine under the hood.

Even on the low-level Clipper, the engine displacement was 320-ci (5.2 L). On the top-level cars, the displacement was 352 (5.7 L). The Ultramatic transmission, combined with the new V-8 and Torsion-Level suspension, made an excellent drive train. The Caribbean, capable of 275 hp, was a powerful car.

Equal to all this was the styling. A careful face-lift of Reinhart's 1951 design, the 1955 Packard wore 'cathedral' taillights, peaked front fenders and a fairly ornate grille. It was a car in the remembered tradition. Unfortunately, there were production line tie-ups and problems with quality control, which were all very detrimental to sales. Packard as a company was dying, but as a signature to a long,

Packard was one of America's revered luxury automakers. The company fell on hard times in the postwar period—both monetarily and stylistically.

Above: An illustration of a 1950 Packard Eight Deluxe sedan. A 288-ci (4.7 L) straight-eight engine of 135 hp was mated to either a manual-shift transmission, or Packard's own version of the automatic, the 'Ultramatic Drive' transmission.

Packard styling later emerged a winner with such sleek designs as the 1956 Four-Hundred hardtop coupe shown in the advertisement *at right.* It also featured 'Torsion-Level' ride, a suspension breakthrough that was greatly admired. The engine was a 374-ci (6.1 L) V-8 of 290 hp.

grand history, the 1955 model was a reflection of its glorious past.

The Hudson was an amalgam of postwar streamlining concepts and absolute comfort. Probably the original 'wide body,' the Hudson had a unique 'step down' body design. After stepping down into the car, one would be impressed immediately by the broad, chair-height seats which seemed to engulf the passenger in their luxurious depths. Despite its low, ground-hugging style, there was plenty of head room in the Hudson—plenty of head room and leg room and stretch out room. In short, it was as if the parlor sofa had been picked up and installed in a car. Combined with this was performance that few other cars could match and, indeed, few other cars boasted such comfort as this. Despite the company's clinging to a basic exterior style for six years, the Hudson was extremely aerodynamic for its time.

The Fairlane Victoria was one of Ford's most sought-after models. Introduced in 1955, it featured special chromework on the sides and was, in fact, Ford's top trim level car. The Crown Victoria featured hardtop styling with a crown molding of chrome that ran up before the rear window and across the roof. *At left:* A 1955 Ford Fairlane Crown Victoria sedan.

Above: A 1956 Ford Fairlane Victoria two-door hardtop. The top engine available for this model was Ford's 200-hp, 292-ci (4.7 L) V-8. Fairlane Victoria V-8 models had dual exhausts.

HOT WHEELS

Speed was a byword of the 1950s. In retrospect, it is sometimes hard to understand why. The average driver had no real need for a car that would run at speeds in excess of 80 mph, but it was a fact: the public craved speed, and that was what it got. Several cars were notoriously fast. Sometimes owners of a certain model year gained a reputation as 'speed demons.' One such car was the 1958 DeSoto Firedome.

DeSoto, one of Chrysler's lines, was a fine, basic family car of the early 1950s. In those years, all DeSotos had six-cylinder engines, running from 236.7 to 250.6-ci (2.74 L). Maximum horsepower was about 116. Then, in 1952, DeSoto came out with the hemi-head Firedome V-8 engine, which developed 160 hp at 4400 rpm. This was the first step in the evolution of DeSoto as a real powerhouse automobile. The Firedome V-8 outsold DeSoto's other models by a margin of 2:1. No one needed further proof that the Firedome was a step in the right direction. Horsepower climbed with each succeeding model year, from 160 in 1952 to 230 and 255 in 1956, when it seemed that the engineers must have reached the limit of engine performance. The next year the top of the line would deliver 290 hp, while the lowest priced model, the Firesweep, roared along with 260 hp.

The DeSoto reached its peak in 1958. Models that year featured a fast-shifting, Torqueflite automatic transmission and torsion bar suspension. The Firedome's optional 305 hp engine could go from zero to 60 in 7.7 seconds. In 13.5 seconds, the speedometer would hit 80 mph, and in less than a minute, the car could be traveling at 115 mph with no sweat at all. What was the lure of such speed outside a race track? Part of it was the new super highways, which had come into being during Eisenhower's term of office. And part of it was the sheer thrill of power. Most people never really attempted to drive their cars 'flat out' anyway, but there was a deep satisfaction in knowing that if you needed the power, it was there.

Buick celebrated its golden anniversary in 1953. Long known for performance and high quality, the Buick of the 1950s was something of the best and the worst of the time.

Buicks of the 1950s were big and powerful. Stylistically, they were bulbous and often ugly. However, in line with the trend toward the fast car, Buick produced its share of exciting automobiles. Most notable of the fast Buicks was

Below: A 1953 Buick Skylark, a limited-edition car with real wire wheels and a 188-hp, 322-ci (5.2 L) V-8, mated to a Dynaflow automatic transmission.

Opposite: A 1958 Buick Special convertible. Cars like this epitomized the glitzy side of the 1950s: they were large and dazzling to the eye.

the Century. The Buick Century of 1954 had a 195 hp V-8 engine coupled with the smaller, lighter body of the Buick Special. It took hardly any time at all for the stock car racers to realize that here was a hot little car capable of scoring big on the tracks. Naturally, General Motors was willing to take advantage of this image. Buick sales soared and horsepower was increased in subsequent years.

In 1956, the Buick Special could deliver 220 hp; the Century provided a hairy 255 hp. There wasn't a single Buick built in that year that couldn't exceed 100 mph. The fiery Century could go from zero to 60 mph in 10.5 seconds and could easily exceed 100 mph. By the time the 1950s drew to a close, the most powerful Buick featured a 401-ci (6.5 L) V-8 engine with a capacity of 325 hp. But the age of the big overpowered car was fading. In that year, 1959, the little German Opels were capturing an increasing part of the market. The handwriting was on the wall.

Of all the automobile makes still in production today, the Oldsmobile is the oldest in the United States. At the turn of the century, people were humming a popular song called, *My Merry Oldsmobile*. The first Oldsmobile was built by Ransom Eli Olds in 1897, whose ambition was to build a car 'in as perfect a manner as possible.'

When William Durant formed General Motors in 1908, the infant company absorbed Oldsmobile. For many years afterward, however, the Oldsmobile was still produced by the Olds Motor Works. Not until World War II did Oldsmobile become officially known as the Oldsmobile Division of General Motors. At GM, the Oldsmobile led the pack in technological innovation. From the Hydra-Matic transmission first introduced on its 1940 models to the overhead-valve Rocket V-8 engine in 1949, Oldsmobile represented the best of GM engineering.

Sherrod Skinner's decision to use the OHV Rocket V-8 in the Olds Eighty-Eight was nothing short of genius. The Eighty-Eight, which weighed 300 to 500 pounds less than the Ninety-Eight, became one of the best racing cars of the early 1950s. Against such formidable contestants as Lincoln, Cadillac and Hudson, the Olds Eighty-Eight proved itself time and again. The horsepower produced by this early Rocket V-8 engine was 165—not bad for a newcomer. Engineers continued to perfect that engine, following the tenets of RE Olds.

By 1954, the lowest output of an 'Olds' engine was 170 hp, and it continued to climb. Two years later, horse-

Opposite, top: A 1956 DeSoto Fireflite Sportsman hardtop. Like many cars of its era, this auto had a fairly potent engine— a 225-hp, 330-ci (5.4 L) V-8.

Also like other makes, DeSoto Fireflites increased in power as the decade matured. *Opposite, middle:* A 1959 DeSoto Fireflite. This car's power plant was a 325-hp, 383-ci (6.2 L) V-8.

In 1958, Chrysler Corporation discontinued their fabulous, 392-ci (6.4 L) 'hemi' V-8—ostensibly, to 'de-emphasize racing.' Paradoxically, they replaced the 'hemi' with an even larger V-8 of conventional design.

Opposite, bottom: A 1959 Chrysler New Yorker, which would have been armed with the 'hemi' a year before, but now had a 413-ci (6.7 L), 350-hp V-8—which in the Chrysler 300 series cars delivered 380 hp.

At left: A 1958 DeSoto Firesweep convertible. The Firesweep series represented DeSoto's lowermost trim level. Its power plant was a 280-hp, 350-ci (5.7 L) V-8.

DeSotos were essentially 'poor man's Chryslers.' In the unstable business climate of the late 1950s, such duplication of lines did not pay off, and DeSoto ceased production in 1961.

Even so, one can see from the lines of this car that dramatic spaciousness and uncompromising forward thrust was Chrysler Corporation's late-1950s ideal.

The Chrysler 300 was the hottest production car of the mid-to-late 1950s—with increasingly larger 'hemi' V-8s, they dominated all others.

Below: A 1956 Chrysler 300B hardtop, with a 340-hp, 354-ci (5.8 L) 'hemi.' Such a car set the 1956 world passenger car speed record at 139.9 mph.

Opposite: A 1956 Oldsmobile Super Eighty-Eight Holiday coupe, powered by a 240-hp, 324-ci (5.3 L) V-8.

power output for the Olds was 230 and 240. By 1957, you could get an Olds with a special J-2 Rocket engine which had three two-barrel carburetors and 300 horses under the hood. The Olds Eighty-Eight thus equipped could go from zero to 60 mph in less than eight seconds. By the end of the 1950s, the Super Eighty-Eight came equipped with a 394-ci (6.4 L), V-8 engine, a four-barrel carburetor and a capacity of 315 hp. In the Oldsmobile tradition, the car was highly rated for performance and power. Economy was not a strong point, however, but economy was beginning to matter to buyers–at least a little.

Chryslers of the early 1950s were rather plain, boxy and not especially stylish, yet Chrysler's engineering was

renowned throughout the decade. Chrysler had long featured an excellent six-cylinder engine, but in 1951, company engineers brought out the hemispherical combustion chamber V-8, a very efficient power plant. A 'hemi' could use a lower octane fuel than the non-hemi, yet the power it produced was more than equal to any conventional engine.

Of all the cars produced during the 1950s, the Chrysler was probably the most dominant of the powerful cars. The 'lionhearted Chrysler' was an apt description. In 1953, Chrysler's engineering staff built four special hemis for the Indianapolis 500. All used Hillborn fuel injection and all were capable of developing over 400 hp. Because of a

Below: A 1958 Chrysler 300D two-door hardtop. The was the most powerful of the 1950s Chrysler 300s. It featured a 392-ci (6.4 L) Firepower 'hemi' V-8 of 380 hp (when equipped with the two four-barrel carburetors that were standard that year). However, a factory-optional fuel injection system further boosted the big V-8 to 390 hp. The Torqueflite automatic transmission was standard equipment.

Opposite: The legendary 1955 Chrysler 300. This car dominated NASCAR racing during the mid-fifties.

displacement limit, the engineers were never able to realize the full potential of these engines, which was disappointing. Nevertheless, when the Chrysler 300 came out in 1955, it became one of the pre-eminent cars in NASCAR racing, developing a whopping 300 bhp from a stock engine. The 1955 Grand National was won by Tim Flock driving the rugged '300' over the notorious Daytona course. Chrysler might have continued to dominate NASCAR racing for many years if the Auto Manufacturers Association had not agreed to downgrade racing.

The T-Bird was Ford's contribution to the field of speedy cars. The two-seater Thunderbird first came on the scene in the mid-1950s. It featured a Y-block V-8 engine of 292-ci (4.7 L). Capable of nearly 200 hp, the Thunderbird was an immediate success, both in the showrooms and on the race tracks. Part of the reason was the car's spectacular good looks, the other part was simply its very lively engine.

The car showed its mettle during 'Speed Week' of 1955. Driven by Bill Spear, the Thunderbird proved the fastest car in Class 3 (cars costing less than $4000). During this race at Daytona Beach, the Spear's T-Bird won over such competitors as the Jaguar 120 and numerous Corvettes.

The two-seater was only in production for three years before Ford's styling department brought out the four-passenger model in 1958. The smaller T-Bird had been a beautiful and exciting car, but many manufacturers of the 1950s were biased toward building larger cars. Not too many of the big manufacturers were aware of an underground movement toward smaller, more compact cars, but nonetheless, it was underway—a kind of slow groundswell that would not fully hit the market until the 1960s. Meanwhile, everyone gloried in a 'bigger is better' concept.

The production cars were not the only ones dedicated to speed and power. Speed enthusiasts of the 1950s with a penchant for tinkering with automobiles experimented with

Not only was it an instant classic, but the 1955 Thunderbird *(opposite)* housed the hottest street engine Ford could muster, which at the time was a 193-hp, 292-ci (4.7 L) overhead-valve V-8. This model was so popular that its manufacture was continued even after the 1956 model year began.

While it is hard even today to resist the allure of *any* Thunderbird, the changes that time would bring to the fabulous 'T-Bird' were not immediately lauded by the car's fans.

This page, both: Views of a 1958 Thunderbird. Note the heaviness of its design as compared with the 1955 model. Even so, this was a car that had no trouble gobbling up the road, with its 300-hp, 352-ci (5.7 L) V-8.

The utmost classic hot rod was the highly-altered Model T Ford. Often, just the bucket-shaped passenger compartment would be used in an altogether new vehicle—called a 'Bucket T,' in honor of its origin.

Near opposite: A 'Bucket T' derived from a Model T pickup. Often these bodies were fiberglass reproductions. Matching that light weight to an outrageously potent drivetrain was part of the fun.

The large V-8 in this particular car is equipped with competition-type exhaust headers and a supercharger, boosting its output to at least 800 hp.

The exhaust pipes running along the side were dubbed 'lakes pipes,' as, in the days before drag racing became a sanctioned sport, cars like this were often run on dry lake beds—for which the cars were called 'lakesters.'

A lot could be done with a Ford Model A, too. In fact, the tradition of the 'hot rod roadster' was strong in the 1950s, with Model A bodies and fenders riding on all-new undercarriages, and powered by engines that were only limited by the builder's resources.

Opposite: A beautifully executed Model A hot rod roadster.

At right: An almost-stock-looking 1957 Chevrolet Bel Air. In the tradition of hot rods, one would be hard put to guess what was under its hood—the closest one could come would be that it was *probably* a General Motors power plant.

various forms of engines, automobile bodies and frames. In many small towns it was a local pastime to put together a car that would outrun everyone at the track. Such cars were called 'hot rods.'

A favorite combination for the classic hot rod was to match a Model T body with a tubular steel frame. For power, a V-8 engine was the thing to have. Added to this was heavy duty suspension and oversize rear wheels. The roadster, stripped down to bare essentials, had a style of its own. Each hot rod was a mark of its owner's individualism. No two were ever alike. They were christened with names like the *Black Banana*, *Mongoose*, *The Plague* and *Freight Train*. They were also extremely noisy, which made the neighbors very irritable.

Young 'hot rodders,' of course, could not refrain from 'trying out' these wondrous machines they'd created, so

there were clandestine 'drag races' in the wee hours when the streets were deserted. Some didn't even wait for the streets to be deserted, but went rumbling out in broad daylight, just for the thrill of it. Dry lake beds, as well as city streets, were particularly attractive for drag racers. Local police, of course, frowned on this activity and the participants usually ended up paying a few stiff fines. Still, as hot rodders argued, working on the cars kept everyone out of worse trouble. No one was 'robbing little old ladies' when he was working on his car.

It was Wally Parks who decided to do something to enable enthusiasts to race safely. Parks founded the National Hot Rod Association in an effort to improve the image of hot rodding and to help the drag racers police themselves. Drag racing became more popular as the 1950s progressed. Like the stock car race, it attracted a varied group of participants. Spectators were mostly the young: kids in their teens and twenties. The noise, smoke and smells didn't bother this group at all; they only added to the atmosphere.

Opposite: A 1957 Pontiac Star Chief Custom Bonneville convertible. As a convertible, this was a 'hot' car aesthetically, and with a fuel-injected, 315-hp, 347-ci (5.6L) V-8 under its hood, was 'hot' in another way, as well.

Above: A 1959 Cherolet Bel Air sedan, with the low, wide-finned look that Chevrolet favored that year. While the top Chevrolet engine was a 315-hp, 348-ci (5.7 L) V-8, the Bel Air's top option was a 280-hp version of same.

Near Opposite: A view of the radical fins of a 1959 Buick. For this model year, Buick engines ranged from a 250-hp, 364-ci (5.9 L) V-8 to a 325-hp, 401-ci (6.5 L) V-8.

Above: A 1959 Ford Skyliner hardtop convertible (also see caption, page 21)—optional power plants included a 300-hp, 352-ci (5.7 L) V-8, while the base engine was a 292-ci (4.7 L) unit.

At top: A 1959 Chevrolet Bel Air two-door sedan. To go with the available engines (see caption, page 113), the company offered standard three-speed manual—plus optional overdrive or two optional automatic—transmissions.

Opposite: A 1959 Pontiac Custom Star Chief sedan. With typically clean Pontiac lines, this make's appearance would become cleaner as the new decade began. Its power plant was a 245- or 280-hp (depending on transmission used), 389-ci (6.3 L) V-8.

THE FRUGAL, THE FAST AND THE FINE

As the 1950s began, the auto industry in Europe was slowly recovering from the devastation wrought by World War II. In Germany, for example, the dream of a people's car was finally realized with the Volkswagen Beetle. Although designed in 1939, production on the Beetle didn't begin until 1945, when only 1785 were built. By 1950, production had increased dramatically to 90,038. The Beetle's popularity continued to grow throughout the decade, eventually becoming one of the most popular cars worldwide. Not all European automakers, however, were building a car for the masses. In 1947, Porsche, the company founded by the brilliant designer Professor Ferdinand Porsche, turned its attention to a new project—a sports car that was destined to become a classic, the 356.

Mercedes-Benz was also hard at work, trying to reestablish the position of preeminence it had held prior to the war. The 1950s saw the development of several outstanding Mercedes-Benz touring cars and sports cars, among them the 180, the 220, the 300 and its high-performance variations, the 300S and 300SL.

The European country with the highest interest in sports cars was Great Britain. To most Britons, the MG Midget of the 1930s was *the* sports car, and after the war MG continued that tradition with its MGA. Austin-Healey, Triumph and Jaguar all gave MG a run for its money with their fast, new cars.

Though austerity was the watchword for many automakers during the postwar years, the autos produced by Rolls-Royce remained as luxurious as they ever were. But as custom-built coachwork became increasingly expensive, standardized bodies became more common.

While the British were building luxury and sports cars, the Australians were well on their way to perfecting a uniquely Australian car. After the war, sensing the public's dissatisfaction with imported cars, General Motors-Holden set out to design a car that would meet the needs of the people of Australia. Larry Harnett, then Managing Director at GM-H, determined that the car must be economical and lightweight yet comfortable over long distances.

In 1948, GM-H introduced the 48-215, the precursor to the legendary FJ Holden. Introduced in 1953, the FJ Holden captured the fancy of the people, earning a place in Australian popular culture, along with 'football, meat pies and kangaroos.'

Opposite: **The 1955 Porsche Speedster. The Speedster was a variation of the Porsche 356 coupe that went into production in 1950. The Speedster was conceived as a 'cheap' roadster to cash in on the post-war sports car boom in America. Because of its lack of a roof and its austere two-seat interior, the Speedster was very light and made the most of its 1.5-L (91.5 ci) engine. Criticized by some as looking like an inverted bathtub, the car was very popular at the race tracks and today is one of Porsche's great cult cars.**

These pages: Some more of Germany's important contributions to the world of motoring in the 1950s. The beautifully streamlined Mercedes-Benz 300SL roadster (*below left*) and 300SL gullwing coupe (*below*) are two classic cars of the postwar period. The 300SL had an amazing top speed of 150 mph (241 kph).

Right: The world-famous Volkswagen Beetle. Production of the Beetle began immediately following the end of World War II, but it wasn't until the 1950s that the phenomenal popularity of the car was realized. It wasn't its styling or performance that made it such a success, but its reliability, resilient engine and resistance to corrosion and decay.

British automakers have traditionally produced some of the world's finest sports
cars. Since the 1930s, the MG company's
T-series of sports cars were considered by
many to be the quintessential examples of
the genre. But in the 1950s, some chal-
lengers arrived on the scene. One such
car was the Triumph TR3A (*left*). This model
was a refinement of the TR2 and TR3
models that preceded it. It is powered by
a 2.0-L (122 ci) engine and is easily iden-
tified by its distinctive wide-mouth grille.

Considered by some to be the most attractive of the famous Jaguar XK series, the
XK150 coupe of 1959 (*right*) was powered
by the legendary dual-cam XK engine. The
versatile engine had a 38-year career that
saw it power a variety of vehicles ranging
from single-seat racing cars to power
boats and armored fighting vehicles.

Left: A 1956 Rolls-Royce Silver Cloud saloon. The Silver Cloud was introduced in 1955 as the successor to the Silver Dawn series.

The desirability of Rolls-Royce automobiles was due primarily to the quality, exclusivity and style of their coachwork. Although the highest quality of engineering and construction were maintained, the technical modernity of Rolls-Royce automobiles gradually fell behind the times in the 1950s. It wasn't until the mid-1960s that Rolls-Royce's technical innovations were brought up to the standard of its outstanding coachwork.

Above: The Silver Lady, or the Spirit of Ecstasy, proud mascot borne by nearly all Rolls-Royce motorcars since 1911.

These pages: MG responded to the challenge posed by Triumph and Austin-Healy by developing the MGA, which was introduced in 1955. The first MGAs were equipped with the MG B-series engine but later they acquired a twin-cam engine like that which powered the record-breaking EX 181 in 1957. With the new 1.6-L (97.6 ci) twin-cam engine the MGA could go from zero to 60 mph (97 kph) in under 10 seconds and reach a maximum speed of 114 mph (183 kph).

Owners say that the MGA is quite forgiving for a high-powered sports car. Its predictable high speed cornering characteristics and responsive handling made it an ideal car for race training.

The MGA was MG's premier sports car from 1955 until 1962, when the company announced its replacement—the MGB.

These pages: The FJ Holden saloon. The FJ was a slight revision of the Holden 48-215, the first car designed and built by Australians for Australians. The 48-215 and the subsequent FJ were designed to be lightweight, fuel efficient and comfortable over long distances. It turned out to be just the car Australians were looking for, becoming the biggest selling car of its time in Australia.

The success of the FJ built a reputation for GM-Holden and allowed them to dominate the Australian marketplace for most of the 1950s.

The FJ evolved into the more modern-looking FE Holden in 1956, which in turn was given a minor facelift in 1958 and renamed the FC Holden. Beneath the skin, the 48-215, the FJ, the FE and FC Holden were basically the same car.

INDEX

Alexander, Larry 67
Alexander, Mike 67
Alfa-Romeo 82, 103
American Automobile
    Association 78, 81
Ash, L David 20
Austin-Healy 80, 116
Barr, Harry 15, 16
Barris, George 62, 65
Bonneville, Utah 27, 28, 87, 88
Bourke, Robert E 12, 16, 90, 92
Buick *1*, 12, 15, 25, *69*, *78*
    Centurion *73*
    Century *1*, *14*, 78, 81, 87, *88*,
        102
    LeSabre *24*, 25, *69*
    Skylark *12*, 55, *55*, *100*
    Special *101*, 102
Cadillac 40-41, 44, 65, 81, 95,
    96, 103
    Coupe de Ville 80
    Eldorado 40, 45
    Series 70 Eldorado Brougham
        40, *40*
    Series 62 *41*, 80, *80*, *96-97*
    Sixty Special Fleetwood *38-39*
Caleal, Dick 16, 18
Campbell, Sir Malcolm 87, 88
Carrera Panamericana *see*
    Mexican Road Race
Carrozzeria Touring Company
    (Milan) 46
Century Club 87
Chevrolet 16, 51, *63*, 71
    Bel Air *13*, *14*, 16, *17*, *50*, 51,
        58,   *61*, *88*, *111*, *114*
    Corvette *2*, 15, *49*, *54*, 55, 109
    Golden Bel Air *17*
    Impala *60*, *66*, 68, *73*, *126*, 127
    Master Deluxe *74*
Chrysler Corporation and cars
    15, 27, 30, 33, 40-41, 44, 48,
    103, 104
    Imperial *44-45*, 65
    New Yorker 15, *22*, *102*
    Saratoga 81

300 78, 80, 87, *104*, 106,
    106-107
Cole, Ed 15, 16
Copp, Harley 95
Cord 9
Crusoe, Lewis D 20
Cummings, Bill 24
Cunningham, Briggs 80, 81
Cushenbery, Bill 68, 71
Daytona Beach, Florida 82, 84,
    87, 109
DeSoto 66
    Custom *42*
    Firedome 100
    Fireflite *102*
    Firesweep *27*, *102-103*
Detroit, Michigan 22, 67
Dodge 26, 27, 28, 47, 84
    Custom Royal *9*
    Custom Royal Lancer 47
    La Femme 47
    Royal *87*
    Sierra 26
Duesenberg 9, 95
Durant, William 103
Duryea Brothers 76
Earl, Harley 16, 25, 40
Eisenhower, US President Dwight
    D 10, 100
Exner, Virgil M 15, 27, 44
Ferrari 84
Flock, Tim 87, 106
Ford, Henry 6, 12
Ford, Walter Buell 92
Ford, William Clay 92
Ford Motor Company and cars
    4-5, *6*, 7, 15, 16, 18, 20, 42, 48,
    61, 65, 66, 67, *67*, 70, 82, 87
    Country Squire *18*, 26, 28
    Crestline Country Squire *27*
    Crestline Skyliner *20*, *114*
    Crestline Victoria *48*
    Custom *18*
    Custom Deluxe *7*, *19*
    Customline *21*, *25*
    Custom 300 *6*
    Edsel 20
        Corsair *35*
    Pacer *116*, *117*
        Ranger *116*, *117*, *123*
    Fairlane *6*
    Fairlane Crown Victoria *99*
    Fairlane 500 Skyliner *20*
    Fairlane 500 Sunliner *25*

Fairlane Sunliner *23*
Fairlane Victoria *64-65*, 99, *99*
Galaxie 6
Mainline *4-5*, *35*
Model A 62, *75*, 110, *111*
Model T *110*
Ranch Wagon 26
Thunderbird 51, 52, *52-53*, 55,
    106, *108*, 109, *109*
France, Bill 78, 84
Frick, Bill 80
Gardener, Vince 92
Gardiner, Major Goldie 84
General Motors 9, 12, 37, 92, 103
General Motors-Holden 116, 126
    FJ Holden 116, *126-127*
Grisinger, Buzz 92
Harnett, Larry 116
Haugdahl, Sig 84
Hershey, Frank 19, 20
Hudson 45, 46, 81, 99
    Hornet 45, 81, *82*
    Jet Liner 46
Indianapolis Speedway 76, 78
Jaguar 62, 109, 116, *121*
Johncock, Gordon 78
Kaiser 42
    Dragon 42, 44
Keller, Al 81
Kohlsaat, HH 76
Koto, Holden 16
Kurtis, Frank 124
Lincoln 41, 44, 82, 84, 103
    Capri 42
    Continental Mark V 95, *95*
    Continental Mark III *94*, 95
    Continental Mark II 92, *92*
    Cosmopolitan *86*
    Premier 42, *43*
Loewy, Raymond 12
MacKenzie, Doc 84
McGriff, Hershel 82
Marriott, Frank 87
Mason, George 46
Mercedes-Benz company and
    cars 116, *118-119*
Mercury 42
    Custom *42*
    Montclair *79*
    Monterey *59*, *66*
Mexican Road Race 82, 84
MG company and cars 116,
    121, 125
    MGA 116, *124-125*

Midget 116
Miller, Reese 92
Mobilgas Economy Run 27, 76
Moon Equipment Company 66
Nance, James 44, 98
NASCAR 46, 78, 80, 81, 82, 87,
    106
Nash 46
    Rambler 46, *47*
National Hot Rod Association 67,
    88, 113
Nichols, Marie 42, 122
Olds, Ransom Eli 84, 103
Oldsmobile 84
    Eighty-Eight *10*, 78, 81, *84*, *85*,
        87, 104
    Golden Rocket *72*
    Ninety-Eight *10-11*, 82
    Rocket Eighty-Eight 81, 82
    Super Eighty-Eight Holiday *33*,
        104, *105*
Opel 103
Packard company and cars 37,
    44, 45, 92, 95, 97
    Caribbean 45, 98
    Clipper 45, *46*, 98
    Eight Deluxe *98*, 99
    Four Hundred *98*
    Mayfair 45, *96*
    Patrician *98*
    Speedster 95
Parks, Wally 88, 113
Petty, Lee 87
Plymouth
    Belvedere *30-31*
    Fury *32*
    Sport Fury *30*
Pontiac 55
    Bonneville Custom 37, *38*
    Chieftain 860 Colony *33*
    Chieftain Deluxe *8*
    LeMans 80
    Star Chief *29*, *56-57*, 58, *112*,
        114-115
    Strato-Streak 55
Porsche, Professor Ferdinand
    116
Porsche company and cars 116
    Speedster *117*
    356 116
Rathmann, Dick 81
Reinhart, John 45, 95, 96, 98
Renner, Carl 16
Roberts, 'Fireball' 87

Rolls-Royce 116, *122-123*, 123
Sall, Bob 84
Schindler, Bill 84
Sears Roebuck Company 124
Skinner, Sherrod 82, 103
Smith, Clay 82, 84
Spear, Bill 109
Spring, Frank 46
Starbird, Darryl 67, 68
Stevenson, Chuck 84
Studebaker company and cars
    12, 16, 77, 98
    Commander *90*
    Loewy Coupe 90, 92
    Starliner 90, *91*
Teague, Marshall 81
Thomas, Herb 81
Tremulis, Alex 124
Triumph 116, *120*
Truman, Harry 10
Volkswagen 15, 116, *119*
Walker, George 18, 92
Walters, Phil 82
Watkins Glen, New York 81
Wichita, Kansas 67
Winfield, Gene 67, 68